Table of Contents

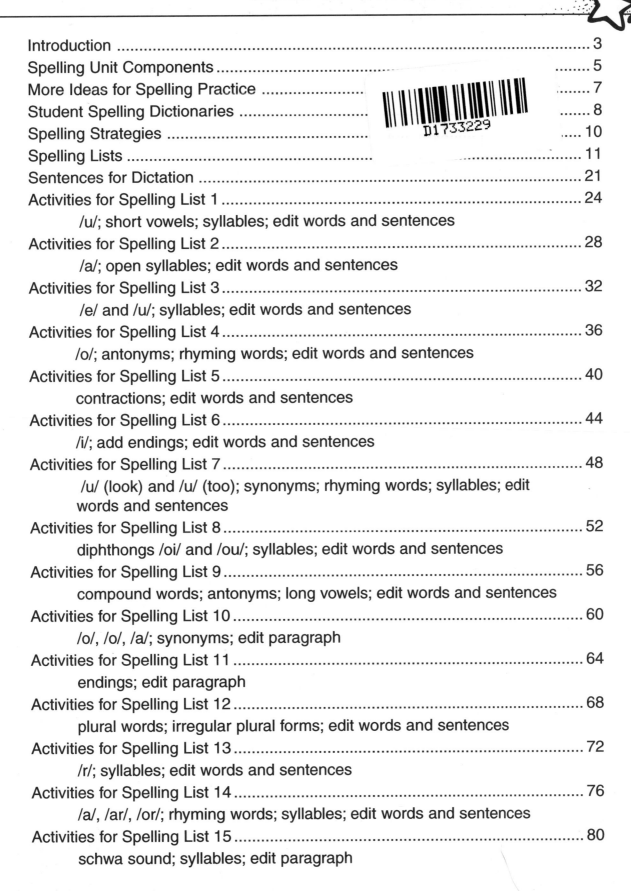

Introduction

Direct Teaching of Spelling

Regardless of the reading philosophy or program used in a school, all students benefit by direct teaching of spelling. This instruction may be a block of time set aside strictly for spelling instruction or an integrated part of a whole language program.

Students need to be taught:

- how to spell words that are created using English phonemes, as well as common non-phonetic words

- learning strategies to help them spell difficult words

- that correct spelling increases their ability to communicate their ideas and feelings to others.

Using This Book

The thirty spelling units contain these components:

- a reproducible list of 18 spelling words

- three sentences for dictation

- four reproducible activity pages for practicing the spelling list words.

A reproducible testing sheet is included on page 146. It contains lines for the 18 spelling words, two special words you may have assigned, three dictation sentences, and three lines that can be used to give review words of your choice from preceding lists.

These components may be placed in a special spelling folder with the student's record sheet *(see page 145)* attached and used as a working portfolio.

Detailed information on each component is given on pages 5 and 6.

The spelling lists can be used for whole-class, small group, or individual instruction. However the lessons are used, start where the students are. Some sixth graders may be ready to skip over the beginning spelling units. (Spelling Grades 3–4 [EMC 726] may be more appropriate for some of your students.)

Following Student Progress
The table of contents contains the skills covered in these spelling lessons. Class and individual record forms (pages 144 and 145) are provided to help you track student progress.

Create Your Own Activities for Spelling Lists
Use the blank forms (pages 147–149) to create spelling lists, word sorts, and crossword puzzles with words from units of study, special holiday words, or words containing a specific phonetic element or skill needing further practice. These forms may also be used to create student-selected spelling lists.

Spelling Unit Components

Lists of Words *(pages 11–20)*

Reproduce the spelling list twice for each student—one copy to use at school and one copy to take home along with the parent letter (page 150).

Students use the list at school for "partner practice" (see page 7), independent practice, and to copy into individual spelling dictionaries (see page 8).

rough
grudge
stunt
thumb
once
another
does
trouble
cousin
began
oxygen
copy
very
until
umpire
sudden
which
city

Sentences for Dictation *(pages 21–23)*

There are three dictation sentences for each spelling list. Space for sentence dictation is provided on the test form (see page 146).

Ask students to listen to the complete sentence as you read it. They then repeat it aloud. Give the sentence in phrases, repeating each phrase one time clearly. Have students repeat the phrase. Wait as students write the phrase.

Repeat with each phrase in the sentence. When the whole sentence has been written, read it again having students touch each word as you say it.

Shorten any sentences you feel are too long or difficult for your students.

Activity Pages

Four reproducible pages are provided for each spelling list. These can be used as teacher-directed lessons, for partner practice, or as individual assignments.

Read, Write, & Spell

This page is used for the initial practice of each spelling word. The student spells one word at a time following these steps:

Step 1 - Read the word and spell it aloud.

Step 2 - Copy the word onto the first blank line and spell it again.

Step 3 - Fold the paper along the fold line to cover the spelling words. (Only the last blank line should be seen.) Write the word from memory.

Step 4 - Open the paper and check the spelling. (This is a <u>very</u> important step. Children need to learn to self-correct so that misspellings are not being practiced.) Repeat the steps for each spelling word.

You may want to write the directions for activity 1 on a chart to post in the classroom.

1. Trace and Spell
2. Copy and Spell
3. Cover and Spell
4. Uncover and Check

2 Word Meaning

Students show an understanding of word meaning by filling in missing words, answering questions, or completing crossword puzzles. Practice includes using compound words, words with multiple meanings, contractions, and homonyms.

(Page 148 contains a form for creating your own crossword puzzles.)

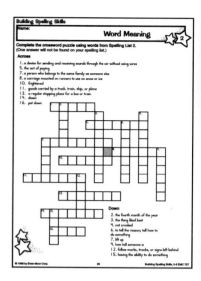

3 Word Study

The phonetic and word-analysis skills on this page may be used for direct-teaching lessons or as independent practice.

Phonics

Students fill in missing phonemes and sort words by sound or spelling patterns.

Word Structure

Practice is provided in using rhyming words, contractions, compound words, syllables, and adding suffixes and prefixes to base words.

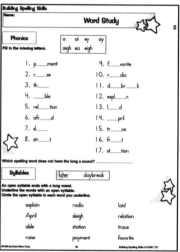

4 Editing for Correct Spelling

Students identify and correct misspelled words in isolation, in sentences, and in paragraphs.

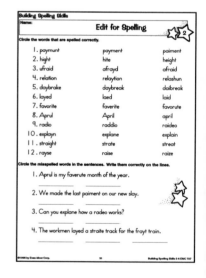

More Ideas for Spelling Practice

Practice with Teacher
Give a pretest to see what type of errors are being made by students. Explain that this is a way to learn what needs to be practiced. It is not a "test" that will be graded in any way. Write each word on a chart or overhead transparency and have students correct their own papers so they can see where they need practice.

Use these errors as a guide for the development of mini-lessons on specific skills or phonemes.

Practice with a Partner
Have students work in pairs to practice their spelling lists. One student gives the word aloud, pronouncing it carefully. The other student writes the word. The "tester" then spells the word aloud as the "writer" checks to see if the word was spelled correctly. Students change roles and repeat the activity.

Extending Use of Spelling Words
1. Have students use the words on their spelling lists in their own writings, both in isolated sentences and in stories and reports.
2. Have students find their spelling words in other places such as posters and charts in the classroom, in literature books, and in magazines or newspapers.
3. Encourage students to find other words that contain the same sound or pattern being studied in the spelling lesson.

Create a Word-Rich Room Environment
You can improve students' spelling by providing a room filled with words.

Provide opportunities for hearing language (talk, tell stories, read to them) and for seeing words (post banners, charts, lists of words, student writings; provide literature books, nonfiction books, magazines, etc.).

Write! Write! Write!
Students' writings serve two purposes. They give the students a chance to use the language and spelling skills they are learning. They provide the teacher with clues to the students' understanding of sound/letter relationships and can help identify which phonetic elements and structural forms need to be practiced.

You will begin to see fewer spelling errors as students transfer new phonetic or structural understandings from the spelling lessons into their writing experiences.

Student Spelling Dictionaries

Self-made spelling dictionaries provide students with a reference for the spelling of words they frequently use in their writing.

Materials to Use:
- copy of "My Own Spelling Dictionary" form (page 9)
- 26 sheets lined writing paper
- 2 sheets construction paper or tagboard for cover - same size as the writing paper
- stapler
- masking tape

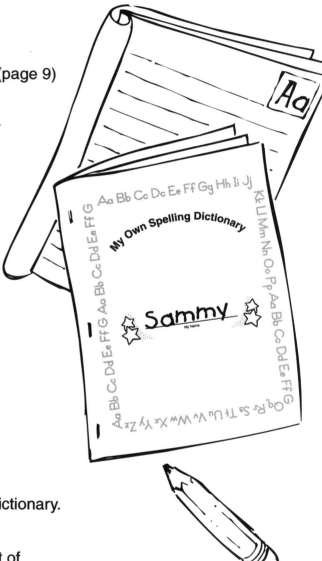

Steps to Follow:
1. Color the cover sheet form. Glue it to the front cover of the dictionary.
2. Staple the lined paper inside the cover. Place masking tape over the staples.
3. Write a letter of the alphabet on each page.

What to Include:
1. When students ask for the correct spelling of a special word, have them write it their dictionary.

2. Include special words being learned as part of science or social studies units.

3. Include words for special holidays.

4. Include words students continue to misspell on tests and in daily written work.

Aa Bb Cc Dc Ee Ff Gg Hh Ii Jj

My Own Spelling Dictionary

_____
Name

Building Spelling Skills 5-6 EMC 727

Spelling Strategies

Learning a few simple strategies can help students become better spellers. Teach the strategies one at a time using appropriate words from the spelling lists. List each strategy on a chart as it is introduced. Post the chart as a helpful reminder to students. Review the strategies frequently to help students internalize them.

Say a word correctly.	Don't leave out or mispronounce sounds. Write the sounds in the correct order.
Think about what the word looks like.	Think about how the spelling pattern looks. Write it, look at it, decide if it looks correct.
Look for small words in spelling words.	spin - pin, in cupcake - cup, cake
Look at syllables in spelling words.	Spell the word one syllable at a time. remember - re•mem•ber
Use rhyming words to help spell a word.	If you can spell book, you can spell look.
Use rules for adding endings.	Drop silent e before adding suffix. Double the final consonant before adding suffix. Change the final y to i and add es.
Use knowledge of suffixes and prefixes.	Think about what the word looks like without the prefix or suffix. Write the word and then add the prefix or suffix.
Think about what the word means.	Some words sound the same, but have different meanings and are spelled in different ways. Match the spelling with its meaning.
Use outside help.	Use words posted around the classroom. Use a dictionary. Ask someone for help.

rough

grudge

stunt

thumb

once

another

does

trouble

cousin

began

oxygen

copy

very

until

umpire

sudden

which

city

afraid

explain

payment

sleigh

laid

raise

straight

freight

height

they

favorite

April

able

radio

station

relation

daybreak

trace

fifteen

referee

eager

easily

ready

please

ecology

maybe

been

only

universe

future

communicate

beautiful

unusual

cute

cube

fuel

Building Spelling Skills 5-6 EMC 727

obey	I'll	idea
ocean	they've	silent
poem	don't	myself
echo	we're	lying
hello	didn't	apply
wrote	isn't	knight
goal	couldn't	quite
approach	haven't	I'm
owner	o'clock	license
tomorrow	you're	buy
program	who's	inquire
broken	whose	higher
potato	aren't	variety
throat	it's	smiling
oldest	doesn't	diagram
followed	there's	rhyme
spoken	won't	widest
awoke	I've	python

Building Spelling Skills 5-6 EMC 727

gloomy	spoil	baby-sit
school	choice	first aid
choose	avoid	flashlight
loose	moisture	high school
route	oyster	goalkeeper
clue	royal	all right
truth	employ	airmail
duty	annoy	one-way
ruin	ground	bodyguard
Tuesday	house	something
usually	sprout	good-bye
threw	mountain	birthday
understood	allow	outside
neighborhood	ourselves	everybody
rookie	somehow	everyone
could	ounce	anything
should	amount	themselves
bulletin	boundary	himself

Building Spelling Skills 5-6 EMC 727

stalk	surrounded	countries
off	skiing	addresses
because	swimming	women
brought	loving	lessons
called	studied	people
drawn	traveling	skis
awful	carried	friends
awkward	trading	roofs
lawyer	bragged	calves
daughter	worried	fences
fault	beginning	flies
author	exciting	lives
always	finished	cherries
already	laughed	businesses
although	quickest	guesses
belong	weaker	families
office	tiniest	leaves
haul	lonelier	pictures

Building Spelling Skills 5-6 EMC 727

urgent	square	about
Thursday	stare	algebra
purpose	dairy	quiet
thirsty	area	other
camera	January	weapon
wonder	dictionary	thousand
smuggler	daring	happen
remember	beware	different
surprise	argument	along
earth	large	equator
certain	partner	hospital
person	guarding	animal
dollar	article	second
color	orchestra	region
collar	ordinary	quarter
early	important	lecture
mayor	force	puncture
doctor	before	again

Building Spelling Skills 5-6 EMC 727

awhile	signal	eagle
where	regular	example
thought	generous	towel
athletes	energy	special
truthful	bridge	legal
purchases	genius	little
exchange	dangerous	whole
though	segment	several
rhythm	figure	terrible
children	country	label
chocolates	circle	question
friendship	concert	frequent
together	peaceful	telescope
white	nice	instead
watches	since	instrument
arithmetic	electric	celebrate
months	dancing	declare
length	decided	address

Building Spelling Skills 5-6 EMC 727

tried

weigh

piece

receive

their

fierce

neither

field

receiving

trying

hurried

siege

weighs

writing

tired

having

planned

worries

kindness

darkness

happiness

loneliness

sadness

weakness

exactly

honestly

speedily

angrily

happily

friendly

especially

teacher

actor

liar

biologist

assistant

scene

they're

through

heir

clothes

byte

aloud

cruise

crews

isle

principal

principle

hour

knew

two

write

chute

reign

thoughtful
successful
wasteful
wonderful
skillful
plentiful
government
amusement
predicament
excitement
punishment
arrangement
fearless
careless
worthless
thoughtless
useless
reckless

shoes
sure
sugar
musician
patience
mission
occasion
physician
tension
conclusion
constitution
caution
constellation
addition
fiction
position
official
glacier

wrestle
wrong
answer
dough
unknown
knapsack
often
listen
climb
half
island
talking
design
scratch
tonight
limb
knot
whistle

Name:

Name:

Name:

rewrite

reappear

recall

recover

rebuild

dishonest

disagree

disappear

disappoint

disconnect

disapprove

misbehave

misfortune

misunderstand

misspell

misuse

illegal

illegible

paragraph

trophy

nephew

enough

cough

fourth

Friday

physical

roughest

pharmacy

fragile

fluid

briefly

festival

stuffed

triumph

telephone

few

imperfect

impolite

impatient

improper

inactive

inconvenient

incorrect

inconsiderate

preview

prejudice

prevent

prefix

prehistoric

unable

uncertain

uncomfortable

unaware

ungrateful

Building Spelling Skills 5-6 EMC 727

geology
geometry
geography
geologist
action
enact
transport
import
portable
bicycle
cyclone
encyclopedia
autograph
automobile
automatic
autobiography
telegraph
photograph

destruct
destruction
describe
description
decorate
decoration
divide
division
administer
administration
populate
population
infect
infection
punctuate
punctuation
attend
attention

multiply
temperature
vertical
equation
currency
amphibian
intersection
environment
agriculture
frequency
civilization
manufacture
characteristic
atmosphere
representative
semicircle
substitute
technology

Sentences for Dictation

List 1
1. The **stunt** diver used an **oxygen** tank **until** he reached the surface.
2. All of a **sudden** my **cousin** was in **trouble** with the **umpire**.
3. They're moving to **another city once** school is out.

List 2
1. The workers **laid** a **straight** track for the **freight** train.
2. **They** listen to their **favorite radio station** at **daybreak**.
3. Can you **explain** why you're **afraid** to remain in the **sleigh**?

List 3
1. In the **future** we may be able to **communicate** with life forms from across the **universe**.
2. Player number **fifteen** was **eager** to hear the **referee's** decision.
3. She was **ready** to buy that **unusual** stone **cube**.

List 4
1. The dog's **owner wrote** a **poem** about his pet.
2. Is the sailor's **goal** to set sail on the **ocean tomorrow**?
3. He **followed** the **oldest** man but didn't **approach** him.

List 5
1. **Who's** going to collect the six **o'clock** mail when **it's** delivered?
2. **Doesn't** he know **they've** already discovered **whose** purse it is?
3. **I've** no idea what **you're** talking about.

List 6
1. **Quite** a large **python** climbed **higher** up into that tree.
2. I found **myself smiling** at the funny **rhyme** about a **knight**.
3. Where do you **apply** to **buy** a fishing **license**?

List 7
1. Kids in my **neighborhood usually choose** to play after **school**.
2. She **understood** the **clue** giving the **route** to the treasure.
3. You **should** be sure to read the **bulletin Tuesday** morning.

List 8
1. It was our **choice** to climb the **mountain** by **ourselves**.
2. Will the **royal** family **employ** me to guard their summer **house**?
3. **Somehow** one **ounce** of **oysters** doesn't seem the right **amount**.

List 9
1. In **high school everybody** learned **something** about **first aid**.
2. The **bodyguard** needs a **flashlight** to find **something outside**.
3. Is it **all right** to send **everyone's birthday** cards **airmail**?

List 10
1. The **lawyer called** home **because** she had to work late.
2. Was it his **fault** that the **awkward** dancer took an **awful** fall?
3. The **author always brought** his work to the editor's **office**.

List 11
1. They were beginning to think the **skiing** trip would be **exciting**.
2. The **tiniest** lady **carried** her own luggage while **traveling**.
3. Both boys **laughed** as they **finished trading** silly riddles.

List 12
1. The **women** gave swimming **lessons** to many **people**.
2. Do you have the **addresses** of your **friends** in other **countries**?
3. One of his **businesses** is taking **pictures** of **families**.

List 13
1. What was the **purpose** of the **mayor's** speech **early Thursday**?
2. The **smuggler** was selling a **camera** for only one **dollar**.
3. Do you **remember** our **surprise** when the **thirsty** dog drank out of the toilet?

List 14
1. An **important article** about **dairy** cows came out in **January**.
2. Why was the police **force guarding** the **orchestra** conductor?
3. Does **ordinary** come **before** or after **square** in the **dictionary**?

List 15
1. A **thousand different** animals live **along** the **equator**.
2. Dr. Hill gave his **second lecture** on treating **puncture** wounds.
3. Is it **quiet** in the **region** of the **hospital**?

List 16
1. The **athletes** trained **together** for **months** before the race.
2. How many **children** made **purchases** of **chocolate** this **month**?
3. I **thought** I would **exchange** my gold **watches** for **white** boots.

List 17
1. **Since** the flood people have been **generous** with time and money.
2. One **segment** of the people at the **concert** was **dancing** in a **circle**.
3. Is it **peaceful** or **dangerous** in that **country**?

List 18
1. **Several** scientists viewed the **eagle** through a **telescope**.
2. I have a **question** about the **address** on that **label**.
3. There was a **special** sale on **towels** for a **whole** week.

List 19
1. The farmer **planned** to **weigh** his crops right in the **field**.
2. King Harry **hurried** to defend the castle from a **fierce siege**.
3. **Neither** worker is **receiving** a **piece** of the profit.

List 20
1. An **actor** must know **exactly** what to do when the stage is plunged into **darkness**.
2. The **biologist's assistant** worked **speedily**.
3. My **teacher** was filled with **loneliness** and **sadness** when her best friend moved away.

List 21
1. Mr. Lee's **heir** spent the money she received on **clothes** and a **cruise**.
2. Our **principal** gave us **two hours** to **write** about the **principles** of good behavior.
3. He **knew** the length of each king's **reign** since the middle ages.

List 22
1. Through **skillful** negotiations, the **government** was **successful** in reaching a solution.
2. Did their **reckless** behavior deserve such a harsh **punishment**?
3. They were filled with **excitement** when the **thoughtful** man made **arrangements** for them to go to the **amusement** park.

List 23
1. On **occasion** the **physician** plays tennis to get rid of **tension**.
2. The **musician** was **sure** hard work and **patience** would pay off.
3. His **official mission** was to map the **position** of **glaciers**.

List 24
1. The boys **often** pack **knapsacks** and camp on the **island**.
2. **Listen** instead of **talking** or you will give the **wrong answer**.
3. Can you **climb** out on that **limb** and **knot** a rope around it?

List 25
1. Do you **recall** when the town had to **rebuild** businesses?
2. You'll have to **rewrite** the story if your handwriting is **illegible**.
3. Father will **disapprove** if we **misbehave** or are **dishonest**.

List 26
1. My **nephew** called on the **telephone** to say that he won a **trophy**.
2. The **roughest physical** activity came on the **fourth** day.
3. A **fragile** girl went to the **pharmacy** for **cough** medicine.

List 27
1. I was **unable** to **preview** the film on **prehistoric** life.
2. Was he **unaware** that his **improper** behavior made us **uncomfortable**?
3. They were **uncertain** how to **prevent prejudice**.

List 28
1. Are you studying **geology, geography**, and **geometry** this year?
2. The **geologist's autobiography** seemed as long an **encyclopedia**.
3. She used an **automobile** to **transport** her largest **photographs**.

List 29
1. Pay **attention** to her **description** of the fire's **destruction**.
2. A new **infection** was spreading through the **population**.
3. Why are they going to **divide** the **administration** into two parts?

List 30
1. Do **amphibians** live in an **environment** with a low **temperature**?
2. Early **civilizations** developed **agriculture** and the use of **currency**.
3. They agreed to **manufacture** signs for the new **intersections**.

Name: _____

Spelling List

1

Read and spell	Copy and spell	Spell and check
1. rough	_____	_____
2. grudge	_____	_____
3. stunt	_____	_____
4. sudden	_____	_____
5. thumb	_____	_____
6. once	_____	_____
7. another	_____	_____
8. does	_____	_____
9. trouble	_____	_____
10. cousin	_____	_____
11. began	_____	_____
12. city	_____	_____
13. oxygen	_____	_____
14. copy	_____	_____
15. very	_____	_____
16. until	_____	_____
17. umpire	_____	_____
18. which	_____	_____
19. _____ (bonus word)	_____	_____
20. _____ (bonus word)	_____	_____

fold

Name:

Word Meaning

Fill in the blanks with words from Spelling List 1.

1. The diver used an _____ tank _____ he reached the surface of the water.

2. My _____ had a _____ against the _____ who called him out.

3. Which _____ did you hurt trying to do that _____?

4. They are moving to _____ _____ next week.

5. All of a _____ it _____ to rain and I got _____ wet.

6. If you _____ his homework you'll get in _____.

Write sentences with these words.

[_____] _____

_____

[_____] _____

_____

         Building Spelling Skills 5-6 EMC 727

Phonics

List the spelling words with the sound of short u.
Then circle the letters that have the short u sound.

_____ r(ou)gh _____ _____ _____

_____ _____ _____

_____ _____ _____

_____ _____ _____

Mark all of the short vowels in these words.

1. begăn   5. umpire
2. opposite   6. which
3. another   7. city
4. copy   8. until

Syllables

Match syllables to make words.
Write the complete word on the line.

1. trou	til	1. _____
2. cous	gan	2. _____
3. be	ble	3. _____
4. cop	y	4. _____
5. un	den	5. _____
6. um	in	6. _____
7. sud	y	7. _____
8. cit	pire	8. _____

Name: _____

Edit for Spelling

Circle the word in each row that is spelled correctly.

1. gruje	grudge	grudje
2. anuther	unother	another
3. does	duz	doez
4. truble	drouble	trouble
5. cuzin	cousin	cuosin
6. oxigun	oxegun	oxygen
7. empare	umpire	umpyre
8. sity	citty	city
9. entil	untill	until
10. which	wich	whitch
11. thum	thumb	tumb
12. very	wery	verie

Circle the misspelled words in the sentences. Write them correctly on the lines.

1. His cuzin lives in unother sity.

   _____ _____ _____

2. The doctor gave the man oxigin entil he begun to breathe on his own.

   _____ _____ _____

3. Wunce I got into truble for doing a silly stunts.

   _____ _____ _____

4. Duz a snake have verie ruff scales on its body?

   _____ _____ _____

Building Spelling Skills

Name: _____

Read and spell	Copy and spell	Spell and check
1. afraid	_____	_____
2. explain	_____	_____
3. payment	_____	_____
4. trace	_____	_____
5. sleigh	_____	_____
6. laid	_____	_____
7. raise	_____	_____
8. straight	_____	_____
9. freight	_____	_____
10. height	_____	_____
11. they	_____	_____
12. favorite	_____	_____
13. April	_____	_____
14. able	_____	_____
15. radio	_____	_____
16. station	_____	_____
17. daybreak	_____	_____
18. relation	_____	_____
19. _____ (bonus word)	_____	_____
20. _____ (bonus word)	_____	_____

fold

Building Spelling Skills 5-6 EMC 727

Name:

Word Meaning

Complete the crossword puzzle using words from Spelling List 2.
(One answer will not be found on your spelling list.)

Across

1. a device for sending and receiving sounds through the air without using wires
5. the act of paying
7. a connection between two or more things
8. a carriage mounted on runners to use on snow or ice
10. frightened
11. goods carried by a truck, train, ship, or plane
13. a regular stopping place for a bus or train
14. dawn
16. put down

Down

2. the fourth month of the year
3. the thing liked best
4. not crooked
6. to tell the reason; tell how to do something
7. lift up
9. how tall someone is
12. follow marks, tracks, or signs left behind
15. having the ability to do something

Name:

Word Study

Phonics

Fill in the missing letters.

a	ai	ey	ay
aigh	ea	eigh	

1. p____ment

2. r____se

3. th____

4. ____ble

5. rel____tion

6. afr____d

7. sl____

8. str____t

9. f____vorite

10. r____dio

11. d____br____k

12. expl____n

13. l____d

14. ____pril

15. tr____ce

16. fr____t

17. st____tion

Which spelling word does not have the long a sound? _____

Syllables

(later   daybreak

An open syllable ends with a long vowel.
Underline the words with an open syllable.
Circle the open syllable in each word you underline.

explain	radio	laid
April	sleigh	relation
able	station	trace
raise	payment	favorite

Name: _____

Edit for Spelling

Circle the words that are spelled correctly.

1.	paymunt	payment	paiment
2.	hight	hite	height
3.	ufraid	afrayd	afraid
4.	relation	relaytion	relashun
5.	daybrake	daybreak	daibreak
6.	layed	laed	laid
7.	favorite	faverite	favorute
8.	Aprul	April	april
9.	radio	raddio	raideo
10.	explayn	explane	explain
11.	straight	strate	streat
12.	rayse	raise	raize

Circle the misspelled words in the sentences. Write them correctly on the lines.

1. Aprul is my faverute month of the year.

_____ _____

2. We made the last paiment on our new slay.

_____ _____

3. Can you explane how a radeo works?

_____ _____

4. The workmen layed a straite track for the frayt train.

_____ _____ _____

Spelling List

3

Read and spell	Copy and spell	Spell and check
1. fifteen		
2. referee		
3. maybe		
4. eager		
5. easily		
6. ready		
7. please		
8. ecology		
9. been		
10. only		
11. cube		
12. universe		
13. future		
14. fuel		
15. communicate		
16. beautiful		
17. unusual		
18. cute		
19. _____ (bonus word)		
20. _____ (bonus word)		

fold

Name:

Word Meaning

Fill in the blanks with words from Spelling List 3.

1. Number _____ was _____ to hear
   the _____'s decision.

2. _____ put that wooden _____ with the
   _____ design on the table.

3. Is the spaceship filled with _____ so it is
   _____ to explore the _____?

4. That is _____ the most _____ painting in
   the museum.

5. Was the speaker able to _____ how important the
   study of _____ is to the _____ of our world?

Write sentences with these words.

Name:

Word Study

3

Phonics

Write the spelling words in the correct boxes.

words with the sound of long e	words with the sound of long u

cube	fifteen	eager	universe	referee	future
easily	ready	please	fuel	maybe	only
cute	ecology	unusual	communicate		

Syllables

Count the syllables in each word.

1. referee _____3_____

2. universe _____

3. maybe _____

4. ecology _____

5. been _____

6. communicate _____

7. beautiful _____

8. unusual _____

9. cube _____

10. easily _____

11. fuel _____

12. fifteen _____

Building Spelling Skills

Edit for Spelling

Circle the word in each row that is spelled correctly.

1. eeger   eager   eagar
2. ready   reedy   reade
3. cute   kute   qute
4. bin   been   bene
5. please   pleaze   pleese
6. butifull   beautuful   beautiful
7. feul   fewl   fuel
8. easily   eesily   eazuly
9. fuchur   fewture   future
10. maybee   maybe   maibee
11. fiftene   fiteen   fifteen
12. coob   cube   kube

Circle the misspelled words in the sentences. Write them correctly on the lines.

1. Plez have the fiftene hats reddy by 5:00.

_____ _____ _____

2. The refree must cumunikate using ownlee signs.

_____ _____ _____

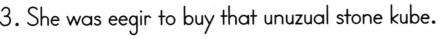

3. She was eegir to buy that unuzual stone kube.

_____ _____ _____

4. Father has bin to the gas station to fewl up the car for our trip.

_____ _____

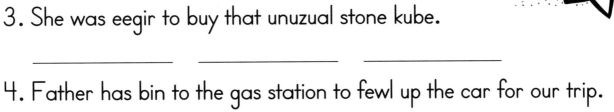

Spelling List

e. slept

4

Read and spell	Copy and spell	Spell and check
1. obey		
2. ocean		
3. poem		
4. awoke		
5. hello		
6. wrote		
7. goal		
8. approach		
9. owner		
10. tomorrow		
11. program		
12. broken		
13. potato		
14. throat		
15. echo		
16. oldest		
17. followed		
18. spoken		
19. _____ (bonus word)		
20. _____ (bonus word)		

fold

Name:

Word Meaning

4

Complete these tasks using the words on Spelling List 4.

1. Write words that rhyme with these words.

a. joke _____

b. wrote _____

c. boldest _____

d. betray _____

e. stole _____

f. loner _____

2. Match the word to its meaning.

a. tomorrow _____ a form of writing that may rhyme,

b. poem _____ one who owns something

c. ocean _____ the day after today

d. goal _____ a listing of what will be performed

e. program _____ a great body of salt water

f. owner _____ a repeated sound made by reflected sound waves

g. echo _____ a result that someone works toward

3. Write the spelling words that are the opposites of these words.

a. disobey _____

b. good-bye _____

c. leave _____

d. youngest _____

e. slept _____

f. led _____

g. repaired _____

Write sentences with these words.

_____

_____

_____

_____

Name:

Word Study

4

Phonics

Circle the letters that have the long o sound.
Now underline the words that have an open syllable.

echo

obey	poem	hello
wrote	goal	ocean
approach	owner	program
tomorrow	broken	potato
throat	oldest	spoken
		awoke

Verb Tense

Circle the correct word or words to show if the verb is present or past tense or both.

1. wrote	present	past	7. approach	present	past
2. broken	present	past	8. obeyed	present	past
3. obey	present	past	9. write	present	past
4. awoke	present	past	10. approached	present	past
5. followed	present	past	11. break	present	past
6. spoken	present	past	12. speak	present	past

Building Spelling Skills

Name: _____

Edit for Spelling

4

Circle the word in each row that is spelled correctly.

1. obay	obey	odey
2. ocean	ochun	osean
3. pome	poam	poem
4. ownar	owner	ownr
5. approach	uproch	upproach
6. rote	wroat	wrote
7. gole	goal	goel
8. putato	patato	potato
9. tomorro	tomarrow	tomorrow
10. program	progrum	porgram
11. troat	throat	throte
12. awoak	woke	awoke

Circle the misspelled words in the sentences. Write them correctly on the lines.

1. The sailor's gole is to set sail on the oshun tomorro.

   _____ _____ _____

2. Did the oldist boy obay the rules?

   _____ _____

3. The borken piece of putato was stuck in his throte.

   _____ _____ _____

4. The dog's onner rote a pome about his pet.

   _____ _____ _____

Building Spelling Skills

Name: _____

Spelling List

5

Read and spell	Copy and spell	Spell and check
1. I'll	_____	_____
2. won't	_____	_____
3. they've	_____	_____
4. don't	_____	_____
5. we're	_____	_____
6. didn't	_____	_____
7. isn't	_____	_____
8. couldn't	_____	_____
9. haven't	_____	_____
10. o'clock	_____	_____
11. you're	_____	_____
12. who's	_____	_____
13. whose	_____	_____
14. aren't	_____	_____
15. it's	_____	_____
16. doesn't	_____	_____
17. there's	_____	_____
18. I've	_____	_____
19. _____ (bonus word)	_____	
20. _____ (bonus word)	_____	

fold

Building Spelling Skills 5-6 EMC 727

Name:

Word Meaning

5

Complete these tasks using words from Spelling List 5.

1. Write the long form of these contractions.

a. o'clock ___of the clock___

b. I've _____

c. won't _____

d. I'll _____

e. they've _____

f. doesn't _____

g. don't _____

h. there's _____

i. we're _____

j. it's _____

k. didn't _____

l. aren't _____

m. you're _____

n. who's _____

o. haven't _____

p. couldn't _____

2. Fill in the missing words.

a. I think _____ too late to go now.

b. He _____ find his homework, and he _____ have time

to look for it.

c. We _____ have enough money for tickets, so we _____

going to the ball game.

d. _____ coming to meet the three _____ train?

Write sentences with these words.

[   ] _____

_____

[   ] _____

Building Spelling Skills

Name: _____

Word Study

Contractions

Write the contraction. Write the missing letters.

1. I will   I'll   w i _____
2. have not   _____   _____
3. we are   _____   _____
4. they have   _____   _____
5. could not   _____   _____
6. you are   _____   _____
7. there is   _____   _____
8. does not   _____   _____
9. it is   _____   _____
10. I have   _____   _____
11. who is   _____   _____
12. do not   _____   _____

Use what you know to write contractions for these words.

1. they are   _____
2. we will   _____
3. would not   _____
4. she has   _____

5. was not   _____
6. they will   _____
7. has not   _____
8. he is   _____

Which two words in List 5 are homophones?

_____   _____

Which homophone goes in this sentence?

Tell me _____ going to the party.

Name:	**Edit for Spelling**

Write the missing apostrophe in the correct place.

1. Ill

2. wont

3. oclock

4. doesnt

5. theres

6. its

7. didnt

8. arent

9. youre

10. havent

Circle the misspelled words in the sentences. Write the words correctly on the lines.

1. Culdn't you fix the broken bike?

_____

2. Who's coat is that?

_____

3. Ive' an idea that theyr'e not coming.

_____   _____

4. Theyv'e traveled to Florida but do'nt have time to visit us.

_____   _____

5. Were going skating. Wo'nt you come with us?

_____   _____

6. Ill try to find out whose going to sing.

_____   _____

Name:

Spelling List

6

Read and spell	Copy and spell	Spell and check
1. idea		
2. silent		
3. lying		
4. apply		
5. knight		
6. quite		
7. I'm		
8. license		
9. buy		
10. inquire		
11. higher		
12. python		
13. variety		
14. widest		
15. smiling		
16. diagram		
17. rhyme		
18. myself		
19. _____ (bonus word)		
20. _____ (bonus word)		

fold

Name:

Word Meaning

Complete the crossword puzzle using words from Spelling List 6.

Across

2. wearing a happy facial expression
3. an official permit
6. a mounted soldier in the Middle Ages
9. a thought
11. what poems often do
12. broadest from side to side
13. a drawing or plan demonstrating something
14. a type of large snake

Down

1. making no sound
4. to ask for information
5. completely
7. at a greater height
8. a number of different types of things
10. making a false statement

Building Spelling Skills 5-6 EMC 727

Name:

Word Study

6

Phonics

Circle the letters that make the long i sound in these words.

1. lying	4. python	7. myself	10. smiling	13. variety	16. higher
2. idea	5. widest	8. apply	11. knight	14. I'm	17. license
3. silent	6. rhyme	9. diagram	12. quite	15. buy	18. inquire

Add Endings

**Write the correct word to complete the sentence.
Then explain how you changed the verb.**

1. Was he _____ or telling the truth?
   (lie)

   explanation: _____

2. Anna _____ as she opened the present.
   (smile)

   explanation: _____

3. The policeman went door to door as he _____ if anyone had
   (inquire)
   seen the accident.

   explanation: _____

4. Who is _____ you those new shoes?
   (buy)

   explanation: _____

       Building Spelling Skills 5-6 EMC 727

Name: _____

Circle the words that are spelled correctly.

1. sylent   5. python   9. hier   13. upply

2. rhyme   6. enquire   10. widist   14. diagram

3. kwite   7. lisence   11. myself   15. smilling

4. bi   8. lying   12. idea   16. knite

Circle the misspelled words in the sentences. Write them correctly on the lines.

1. The knite made a diagarm of the castle's defenses.

   _____ _____

2. I found miself smileng at the silunt movie.

   _____ _____ _____

3. A pyton crawled hier up into the tree.

   _____ _____

4. Im going to bye some of each varitee of candy for the party.

   _____ _____

Name:

Spelling List

7

Read and spell	Copy and spell	Spell and check
1. gloomy		
2. school		
3. choose		
4. loose		
5. route		
6. clue		
7. truth		
8. duty		
9. ruin		
10. Tuesday		
11. usually		
12. threw		
13. understood		
14. neighborhood		
15. rookie		
16. could		
17. should		
18. bulletin		
19. _____ (bonus word)		
20. _____ (bonus word)		

fold

Building Spelling Skills

Name:

Word Meaning

Answer these questions.

1. Which spelling words rhyme with these words?

a. would   _____   d. beauty   _____

b. spool   _____   e. cookie   _____

c. flew   _____   f. booth   _____

2. Which spelling words have about the same meanings as these words?

a. dreary   _____   f. select   _____

b. tossed   _____   g. hint   _____

c. beginner   _____   h. honesty   _____

d. comprehended   _____   i. announcement   _____

e. pathway   _____   j. destroy   _____

Write sentences with these words.

Name:

Word Study

7

Phonics

Write the spelling words in the correct boxes.

/u̇/ - look	/ü/ - too

gloomy	school	clue	choose	loose
duty	rookie	route	ruin	could
bulletin	threw	should	Tuesday	
usually	neighborhood	truth	understood	

Syllables

Match syllables to make words. Write the complete words on the lines.

1. gloom   ie   1. _____

2. rook   in   2. _____

3. du   y   3. _____

4. ru   day   4. _____

5. Tues   ty   5. _____

Edit for Spelling

Name:

Circle the words that are spelled correctly.

1. gloomee   5. klue   9. chosse   13. upply

2. school   6. truth   10. dooty   14. usually

3. rute   7. tuesday   11. bulletin   15. ruin

4. rookie   8. throo   12. shud   16. culd

Circle the misspelled words in the sentences. Write them correctly on the lines.

1. Will the gloome weather rooin our picnic?

   _____   _____

2. I need a klew to who is telling the trooth.

   _____   _____

3. The kids in my nayberhood usully play after skool.

   _____   _____   _____

4. He undrestood the news bulliten.

   _____   _____

51

Name: _____

Spelling List

8

Read and spell	Copy and spell	Spell and check
1. spoil	_____	_____
2. choice	_____	_____
3. avoid	_____	_____
4. moisture	_____	_____
5. oyster	_____	_____
6. royal	_____	_____
7. employ	_____	_____
8. annoy	_____	_____
9. ground	_____	_____
10. house	_____	_____
11. sprout	_____	_____
12. mountain	_____	_____
13. allow	_____	_____
14. ourselves	_____	_____
15. somehow	_____	_____
16. ounce	_____	_____
17. amount	_____	_____
18. boundary	_____	_____
19. _____ (bonus word)	_____	_____
20. _____ (bonus word)	_____	_____

fold

Name: _____

Word Meaning

8

Fill in the blanks with words from Spelling List 8.

1. _____ on the _____ trail made it too wet to climb.

2. The raw _____ will _____ if it's not kept cold.

3. Is one _____ of sugar the right _____ for this recipe?

4. Don't _____ your dogs to _____ the neighbor's cat.

5. Do you think the _____ family would _____ me as a palace guard?

6. A plant began to _____ along the _____ between my yard and the _____ next door.

Write sentences with these words.

_____

_____

_____

_____

_____

       Building Spelling Skills 5–6 EMC 727

Building Spelling Skills

Name: _____

Word Study

8

Phonics

Fill in the missing letters to make spelling words.

oi	oy

1. ch____ce
2. r____al
3. sp____l
4. av____d
5. empl____
6. m____sture
7. ____ster
8. ann____

ou	ow

1. gr____nd
2. h____se
3. b____ndary
4. all____
5. m____ntain
6. ____rselves
7. someh____
8. ____nce

Syllables

Divide these words into syllables.

1. avoid _____ _____

2. oyster _____ _____

3. royal _____ _____

4. employ_____ _____

5. annoy _____ _____

6. mountain _____ _____

7. ourselves _____ _____

8. allow _____ _____

9. somehow _____ _____

10. amount _____ _____

Name: _____

Edit for Spelling

Circle the word in each row that is spelled correctly.

1. spoyl	spoil	spoll
2. royul	royle	royal
3. avode	uvoid	avoid
4. oister	oyster	oystre
5. ounce	ownce	oince
6. amont	amount	umount
7. sumhow	somehou	somehow
8. areselfs	ourselves	ourselfs
9. annoy	unnoy	anoye
10. boundery	boundary	boundry

Circle the misspelled words in the sentence. Write them correctly on the lines.

1. Mr. and Mrs. Ruiz enploy a maid to clean their howse.

   _____ _____

2. It was his choyse to climb to the top of the mountin.

   _____ _____

3. The morning dew left moysture on the grownd.

   _____ _____

4. Sumhow one ownce doesn't seem to be the right umount.

   _____ _____ _____

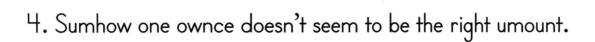

Name:

Spelling List

9

Read and spell	Copy and spell	Spell and check
1. baby-sit	_____	_____
2. first aid	_____	_____
3. flashlight	_____	_____
4. high school	_____	_____
5. goalkeeper	_____	_____
6. all right	_____	_____
7. airmail	_____	_____
8. one-way	_____	_____
9. bodyguard	_____	_____
10. something	_____	_____
11. good-bye	_____	_____
12. birthday	_____	_____
13. outside	_____	_____
14. himself	_____	_____
15. everybody	_____	_____
16. everyone	_____	_____
17. anything	_____	_____
18. themselves	_____	_____
19. _____ (bonus word)	_____	_____
20. _____ (bonus word)	_____	_____

fold

Name:

Word Meaning

Answer these questions using the words on Spelling List 9.

1. There are three ways a compound word can be formed. Study the words in Spelling List 9. Describe the three types of compound words.

    a. _____

    b. _____

    c. _____

2. Which spelling words refer to people?

    _____   _____   _____

    _____   _____   _____

3. What would someone give you if you were injured?   _____

4. Which word names a special day?   _____

5. Which words stand for "all people"? _____   _____

6. Which spelling words have the opposite meaning to these words?

    hello   _____

    nothing   _____

    inside   _____

    nobody   _____

Write sentences with these words.

	_____

_____

	_____

_____

Word Study

9

Name:

Compound Words

Use one word from each box to make compound words.
Cross out each word as you use it.
Check Spelling List 9 to make sure that you form the compound words correctly.

1	2
out	thing
birth	bye
high	self
good	mail
him	right
some	day
all	school
air	side

_____

_____

_____

_____

_____

_____

_____

Phonics

Circle the letter or letters that make the long vowel sounds in the words below. Then circle the sound that the letter or letters make. Some words will have two long vowels circled.

	a	e	i	o	u
1. first aid	ⓐ	e	i	o	u
2. flashlight	a	e	i	o	u
3. one-way	a	e	i	o	u
4. everyone	a	e	i	o	u
5. maybe	a	e	i	o	u
6. anything	a	e	i	o	u
7. baby-sit	a	e	i	o	u

Building Spelling Skills

Name: _____

Edit for Spelling

Circle the word in each row that is spelled correctly.

1. baby sit	babysit	baby-sit
2. first aid	firstaid	first-aid
3. flash light	flashlight	flash-light
4. all right	allright	all-right
5. air mail	airmail	air-mail
6. one way	oneway	one-way
7. birth day	birthday	birth-day
8. good bye	goodbye	good-bye
9. any thing	anything	any-thing
10. high school	highschool	high-school

Circle the misspelled words in the sentences. Write them correctly on the lines.

1. The coach gave first-ade to the injured goal keeper.

   _____ _____

2. Is it allright to send the birth day card air-mail?

   _____ _____ _____

3. The bodygard used a flashlite to find his way in the dark.

   _____ _____

 4. Evrybody is playing out side on the lawn.

   _____ _____

 Building Spelling Skills 5-6 EMC 727

Name: _____

Spelling List

10

Read and spell	Copy and spell	Spell and check
1. stalk	_____	_____
2. off	_____	_____
3. because	_____	_____
4. brought	_____	_____
5. called	_____	_____
6. drawn	_____	_____
7. awful	_____	_____
8. awkward	_____	_____
9. lawyer	_____	_____
10. daughter	_____	_____
11. fault	_____	_____
12. author	_____	_____
13. always	_____	_____
14. already	_____	_____
15. although	_____	_____
16. belong	_____	_____
17. haul	_____	_____
18. office	_____	_____
19. _____ (bonus word)	_____	_____
20. _____ (bonus word)	_____	_____

fold

Building Spelling Skills 5-6 EMC 727

Name:

Word Meaning

10

Fill in the blanks with words from Spelling List 10.

1. The queen's _____ felt _____ when she spilled her lunch on the floor.

2. Has the _____ of the book _____ the illustrations also?

3. The _____ was _____ in his _____ by 7 o'clock this morning.

4. Grandmother _____ _____ presents when she came to visit us.

5. The picnic was _____ off _____ of the rain.

Write sentences with these words.

_____

_____

_____

_____

_____

_____

Building Spelling Skills

Name: _____

Phonics

Circle the letters that have the same vowel sound that you hear in ball.

1. stalk
2. off
3. because
4. brought
5. called

6. drawn
7. haul
8. belong
9. office
10. although

11. awkward
12. already
13. daughter
14. lawyer
15. author

Synonyms

Write the spelling words that are synonyms for these words.

1. terrible _____
2. clumsy _____
3. mistake _____
4. writer _____

5. forever _____
6. be suitable _____
7. carry _____
8. away _____

Complete the sentences.

1. The _____ dancer tripped over her own feet and had
   (clumsy)

   an _____ fall.
   (terrible)

2. My favorite _____'s work will last _____ .
   (writer)   (forever)

3. Did you _____ the junk _____ to the dump?
   (carry)   (away)

Name:

Edit for Spelling

Circle the 11 misspelled words below. Write them correctly on the lines.

Mrs. Bernard, the lawyre, colled home to say she wouldn't be home for dinner becawse she had work to do. She ask her dotter to bring her something to eat at the ofice.

Alice brote her mother some soup and salad. While she was pouring the soup, the awkword girl spilled it all over the papers on her mother's desk.

Alice felt awfull. She knew her mother had draun up the papers for a client who was coming to sign them in the morning.

Her mother said, "It's your fawlt the papers are ruined, but I know it was an accident. Don't worry. I all ways save a copy of important papers on my computer. I will print out a new set after dinner. Now, let's clean up the mess and eat."

_____   _____   _____

_____   _____   _____

_____   _____   _____

_____   _____

Name:

Spelling List

11

Read and spell	**Copy and spell**	**Spell and check**
1. surrounded		
2. skiing		
3. swimming		
4. loving		
5. studied		
6. traveling		
7. carried		
8. trading		
9. bragged		
10. worried		
11. beginning		
12. exciting		
13. finished		
14. laughed		
15. quickest		
16. weaker		
17. tiniest		
18. lonelier		
19. _____ (bonus word)		
20. _____ (bonus word)		

fold

Building Spelling Skills 5-6 EMC 727

Name:

Word Meaning

11

Complete these tasks using the words on Spelling List 11.

1. Write the verbs that are past tense.

_____   _____   _____

_____   _____   _____

_____   _____   _____

2. Which words name activities you can do outdoors?

_____   _____

3. Write the word that means:

a. completed a task   _____

b. going from one place to another   _____

c. not as strong as someone else   _____

d. concerned about something   _____

e. the fastest one   _____

f. made a happy sound   _____

g. talked about how good you are   _____

h. the smallest one   _____

Write sentences with these words.

_____

_____

Building Spelling Skills

Name: _____

Word Study

11

Word Endings

Add ing **to the base words.**
Check how you changed the word.

	no change	drop e add ing	double final consonant
1. laugh _____			
2. love _____			
3. begin _____			
4. ski _____			
5. swim _____			

Add ed **to the base words.**
Check how you changed the word.

	no change	change y to i and add ed	drop e and add ed
1. surround _____			
2. study _____			
3. trade _____			
4. carry _____			
5. excite _____			

Add Endings

Add er **or** est **to each verb to make a comparison.**

1. A cheetah is the _____ member of the cat family.
   (quick)
2. I was _____ than anyone else at camp.
   (lonely)
3. Matthew was _____ than anyone else in nursery school.
   (weak)
4. A hummingbird is the _____ bird.
   (tiny)

| Name: | **Edit for Spelling** |  |

Circle the 9 misspelled words below. Write them correctly on the lines.

George braged about how great he was at sking. He laffed at the other skiers at the begining of the downhill race. He was sure he would win.

It was exsiting swooping down the slopes. Halfway through the race George became worred. Although he was travling as fast as he could, he was not the qwickest racer.

George was very upset when he finish last. "I'll never brag before a race again," he cried.

_____   _____   _____

_____   _____   _____

_____   _____   _____

Name: _____

Spelling List

12

Read and spell	Copy and spell	Spell and check
1. countries	_____	_____
2. addresses	_____	_____
3. women	_____	_____
4. lessons	_____	_____
5. people	_____	_____
6. skis	_____	_____
7. friends	_____	_____
8. roofs	_____	_____
9. calves	_____	_____
10. fences	_____	_____
11. flies	_____	_____
12. lives	_____	_____
13. cherries	_____	_____
14. businesses	_____	_____
15. guesses	_____	_____
16. families	_____	_____
17. leaves	_____	_____
18. pictures	_____	_____
19. _____ (bonus word)	_____	_____
20. _____ (bonus word)	_____	_____

fold

Name:

Word Meaning

Complete the crossword puzzle using words from Spelling List 12.

Across

4. more than one adult female
5. the parts of a tree that make its food
6. places where mail is directed
8. more than one person
12. two long runners used to go down snowy hills
14. sweet round fruits
15. small flying insects
16. commercial establishments

Down

1. several nations
2. more than one baby cow
3. opinions formed without exact knowledge
5. things to be learned
7. railings or walls around yards
9. people who know and like each other
10. groups of relatives
11. more than one life
13. coverings over buildings

Building Spelling Skills

Name: _____

Word Study

12

Plural Nouns

Change each singular noun to its plural form. Check how you changed the word.

	add s or es	change y to i and add es	change f to v and add es
1. ski _____			
2. country _____			
3. fence _____			
4. leaf _____			
5. roof _____			
6. fly _____			
7. life _____			
8. family _____			
9. guess _____			
10. picture _____			
11. calf _____			
12. lessons _____			

Irregular Plurals

Write the irregular plural nouns for these words.

1. woman _____

2. cactus _____

3. mouse _____

4. octopus _____

5. ox _____

6. moose _____

7. deer _____

8. foot _____

Building Spelling Skills

Name: _____

Edit for Spelling

Circle the words that are spelled correctly.

countrys	addresses	womun	lessons
peeple	skiis	friends	cherrys
rooves	leaves	calfs	fences
flys	families	lifes	businesses

Circle the misspelled words in the sentences. Write them correctly on the lines below.

1. The two womun taught swimming lessuns to many peopel.

   _____ _____ _____

2. I have the adresses of many frends living in countrys around the world.

   _____ _____ _____

3. One of Mr. Lewis's busnesses is taking pitchers of familees.

   _____ _____ _____

4. His calfs became ill after eating green cherrys.

   _____ _____

   Building Spelling Skills 5-6 EMC 727

Name:

Spelling List

13

Read and spell	Copy and spell	Spell and check
1. urgent		
2. Thursday		
3. purpose		
4. thirsty		
5. camera		
6. wonder		
7. smuggler		
8. remember		
9. surprise		
10. earth		
11. certain		
12. person		
13. dollar		
14. color		
15. collar		
16. early		
17. mayor		
18. doctor		
19. _____ (bonus word)		
20. _____ (bonus word)		

fold

Name:

Word Meaning

13

Complete the crossword puzzle using words from Spelling List 13.
(There is one word in this puzzle that is not on your spelling list.
See if you can figure out that answer.)

Across
3. sure about something
6. the opposite of forget
11. the opposite of hot
12. a healer of sick people
14. something unexpected
15. the day after Wednesday

Down
1. an instrument used to take photographs
2. reason for doing something
4. the planet we live on
5. a person who brings things into the country illegally
7. person who heads a city or town government
8. red, yellow, blue, etc.
9. to be curious about something
10. needing a drink of water
11. the part of a shirt that is around the neck
12. a piece of money worth 100 cents
13. a human being

Name:

Word Study

13

Phonics

Circle the letters that stand for the /ər/ sound.

urgent	Thursday	smuggler
thirsty	earth	surprise
collar	certain	person
camera	color	dollar
wonder	purpose	early
doctor	mayor	

How many ways was /ər/ spelled? _____

Syllables

Match syllables to make spelling words.
Write the complete words on the lines.

1. ur	y	1. _____urgent_____
2. thirst	gler	2. _____
3. won	gent	3. _____
4. smug	ly	4. _____
5. pur	tain	5. _____
6. col	der	6. _____
7. cer	pose	7. _____
8. may	prise	8. _____
9. ear	lar	9. _____
10. sur	or	10. _____

Name: _____

Edit for Spelling

13

Correct the spelling of the sound /ər/ in these words.

ar	or	ur	ir	er	ear

1. irgent _____

2. camira _____

3. irth _____

4. dollir _____

5. wondir _____

6. mayir _____

7. pirson _____

8. doctir _____

9. irly _____

10. colir _____

Circle the misspelled words in the sentences. Write them correctly on the lines.

1. The mayir gave a speech erly Thirsday morning.

_____   _____   _____

2. It's irgent that the thirstee man gets water quickly.

_____   _____

3. I'm cirtain the docter can help me.

_____   _____

4. Did that persun remembre the perpose of our meeting?

_____   _____   _____

5. A smugglar tried to sell a stolen kamera for one doller.

_____   _____   _____

Name:

Spelling List

14

Read and spell	**Copy and spell**	**Spell and check**
1. square		
2. stare		
3. dairy		
4. area		
5. January		
6. dictionary		
7. daring		
8. beware		
9. argument		
10. large		
11. partner		
12. guarding		
13. article		
14. orchestra		
15. ordinary		
16. important		
17. force		
18. before		
19. _____ (bonus word)		
20. _____ (bonus word)		

fold

Name: _____

Word Meaning

14

Answer the questions using words from Spelling List 14.

1. **What would you use to look up the meaning of a word?** _____

2. **Where is milk put into bottles?** _____

3. **What do you call...**

   a. a large group of musicians playing together? _____

   b. a person you team up with? _____

4. **Which spelling word means...?**

   a. be careful _____   d. protecting _____

   b. brave _____   e. power _____

   c. disagreement _____

5. **Which spelling word is an antonym for...?**

   a. small _____

   b. after _____

   c. unique _____

6. **Which spelling word rhymes with...?**

   a. stare _____   d. barge _____

   b. wearing _____   e. horse _____

   c. declare _____   f. adore _____

Write sentences with these words.

_____

_____

_____

_____

Name:

Word Study

14

Phonics

Write the words in the correct boxes.

words with the sound of /a/ in fair	words with the sound of /ar/ in car	words with the sound of /or/ in store

square   argument   orchestra   dairy
stare   large   ordinary   area
important partner   guarding   force
January   dictionary   article   daring
before   beware

Syllables

Fill in the missing syllables.

1. argu_____

2. be_____

3. _____ner

4. or_____tra

5. im_____tant

6. dic_____ary

7. ar_____cle

8. _____fore

9. ordi_____y

10. dar_____

Name: _____

Edit for Spelling

14

Circle the words that are spelled correctly.

skware	stare	derry
partner	bewear	article
larje	forse	orchestra
befor	area	january
dicshunary	daring	argument
garding	ordinery	importent

Circle the misspelled words in the sentences. Write them correctly on the lines.

1. Members of the police fource were garding the orkestra conductor.

   _____ _____ _____

2. An inportant artikle was in the newspaper last january.

   _____ _____ _____

3. Bewair of argumints with lawrge strangers.

   _____ _____ _____

4. That green areeu is called the town sqware.

   _____ _____

Building Spelling Skills

Name: _____

Spelling List

15

Read and spell	Copy and spell	Spell and check
1. about	_____	_____
2. algebra	_____	_____
3. quiet	_____	_____
4. other	_____	_____
5. weapon	_____	_____
6. thousand	_____	_____
7. happen	_____	_____
8. different	_____	_____
9. along	_____	_____
10. equator	_____	_____
11. hospital	_____	_____
12. animal	_____	_____
13. second	_____	_____
14. region	_____	_____
15. quarter	_____	_____
16. lecture	_____	_____
17. puncture	_____	_____
18. again	_____	_____
19. _____ (bonus word)	_____	_____
20. _____ (bonus word)	_____	_____

fold

Building Spelling Skills 5-6 EMC 727

Name:

Word Meaning

15

Fill in the blanks with words from Spelling List 15.

1. The climate along the _____ is very _____ from the climate in Alaska.

2. She went to the _____ to have a wild _____ bite treated by a doctor.

3. I am taking _____ as my math class next this year.

4. Do you know what will _____ if you do that _____?

5. Please fix the _____ in my bike's tire.

6. I go to the _____ nearest the river when I need peace and _____ .

7. The _____ at the library cost only a _____ .

Write sentences with these words.

```
┌──────────────┐
│              │   _____
└──────────────┘
   _____

┌──────────────┐
│              │   _____
└──────────────┘
   _____
```

Building Spelling Skills 5-6 EMC 727

Name: _____

Word Study

15

Phonics

Put the symbol ə over the letter or letters that have the schwa sound.

ə
about

algebra	brother	weapon
thousand	happen	animal
along	hospital	second
region	again	

Syllables

Divide these words into syllables.

1. about _____ _____

2. other _____ _____

3. weapon _____ _____

4. happen _____ _____

5. along _____ _____

6. region _____ _____

7. quarter _____ _____

8. second _____ _____

9. lecture _____ _____

10. puncture _____ _____

11. thousand _____ _____

12. quiet _____ _____

13. algebra _____ _____ _____

14. different _____ _____ _____

15. equator _____ _____ _____

16. hospital _____ _____ _____

17. again _____ _____

18. animal _____ _____ _____

Name:

Edit for Spelling

Circle the 13 misspelled words below. Write them correctly on the lines.

It was kwiet in the jungle. Tomas huddled like a scared animle in the brush. He had come to this rejun to give a lechure ubout using rainforest plants in medicine. But now he was stranded on a deserted, unpaved road somewhere near the equater. A tire on his vehicle was puntured, and the vehicle was stalled on the side of the road. He had no weppon and a broken leg, and it was almost dark.

What would hapen next? Only a few travelers had passed him allong the road as he had driven toward the field hospitel, where he was to have spoken. Now, if he ever made it to his destination, instead of speaking, he would be a patient. As the secunds dragged by, Tomas peered down the road agin and then slipped into unconsciousness.

_____   _____   _____

_____   _____   _____

_____   _____   _____

   _____   _____

_____   _____

Name: _____

Spelling List

16

Read and spell	Copy and spell	Spell and check
1. awhile	_____	_____
2. where	_____	_____
3. thought	_____	_____
4. athletes	_____	_____
5. truthful	_____	_____
6. purchases	_____	_____
7. exchange	_____	_____
8. though	_____	_____
9. rhythm	_____	_____
10. children	_____	_____
11. chocolates	_____	_____
12. friendship	_____	_____
13. together	_____	_____
14. white	_____	_____
15. watches	_____	_____
16. arithmetic	_____	_____
17. months	_____	_____
18. length	_____	_____
19. _____ (bonus word)	_____	_____
20. _____ (bonus word)	_____	_____

fold

Building Spelling Skills

Name:

Word Meaning

Answer the questions using words from Spelling List 16.

1. What is the plural form of these nouns?

a. athlete _____   c. child _____

b. watch _____   d. chocolate _____

2. Which word has both these meanings?

a. buys things **and**
   the things you buy   _____

b. looks at something **and**
   timepieces worn on your wrist   _____

c. a place where stocks are bought
   and sold **and** to trade things   _____

**3. Which spelling word describes one
   thing dancers and musicians need?**   _____

4. Which words contain the digraph /th/?
   Circle every /th/ that has the sound you hear in thin.

_____ _____ _____

_____ _____ _____

_____ _____ _____

5. Which spelling words rhyme with these words?

a. smile _____   d. slow _____

b. bear _____   e. range _____

c. caught _____   f. sight _____

Building Spelling Skills

Name: _____

Word Study

Phonics

| wh | ch | tch | sh | th |

Fill in the missing digraphs.

1. a____ile
2. ____ought
3. ex____ange
4. rhy____m
5. ____ocolates
6. wa____es

7. ____ere
8. a____letes
9. tru____ful
10. pur____ases
11. ____ough
12. friend____ip

13. leng____
14. ____ite
15. ____ildren
16. ari____metic
17. mon____s
18. toge____er

Plural Nouns

Write the plural form of each noun.

1. month _____
2. athlete _____
3. child _____

4. chocolate _____
5. watch _____
6. purchase _____

Using what you know about forming plural nouns, circle the irregular plural nouns in this list.

cities   women

sleighs   skis

radios   families

countries   children

potatoes

Name: _____

Edit for Spelling

Circle the words that are spelled correctly.

athletes	rythm	together
troothful	awhile	childern
choclates	length	purchasis
though	frendship	exchange

Circle the misspelled words in the sentences. Write them correctly on the lines.

1. Both atheletes trained for munths before the track meet.

   _____ _____

2. Did the childrn study for their arithmutic test?

   _____ _____

3. How many perchases of choclates were made on Saturday?

   _____ _____

4. Our frendship has lasted a long time, even thought we argue
   sometimes.

   _____ _____

5. I'm going to exchanj my gold waches for wite leather boots.

   _____ _____ _____

Building Spelling Skills

Name: _____

Spelling List

Read and spell	Copy and spell	Spell and check
1. signal	_____	_____
2. regular	_____	_____
3. generous	_____	_____
4. energy	_____	_____
5. bridge	_____	_____
6. genius	_____	_____
7. dangerous	_____	_____
8. segment	_____	_____
9. figure	_____	_____
10. country	_____	_____
11. circle	_____	_____
12. concert	_____	_____
13. peaceful	_____	_____
14. nice	_____	_____
15. since	_____	_____
16. electric	_____	_____
17. dancing	_____	_____
18. decided	_____	_____
19. _____ (bonus word)	_____	_____
20. _____ (bonus word)	_____	_____

fold

Building Spelling Skills

Name: _____

Word Meaning

Complete the crossword puzzle using words from Spelling List 17.

Across

3. made up your mind
4. a perfectly round shape
6. something built over a river so people and vehicles can go across
7. a form or shape
9. the opposite of selfish
12. from then till now
13. a part of the whole thing
14. happening again and again at the same time
15. pleasing, agreeable
16. land, nation, region

Down

1. signs giving notice of something
2. free from strife; calm
3. the opposite of safe
5. the capacity for doing work
8. an exceptionally intelligent or gifted person
10. charged with electrical energy
11. a musical performance

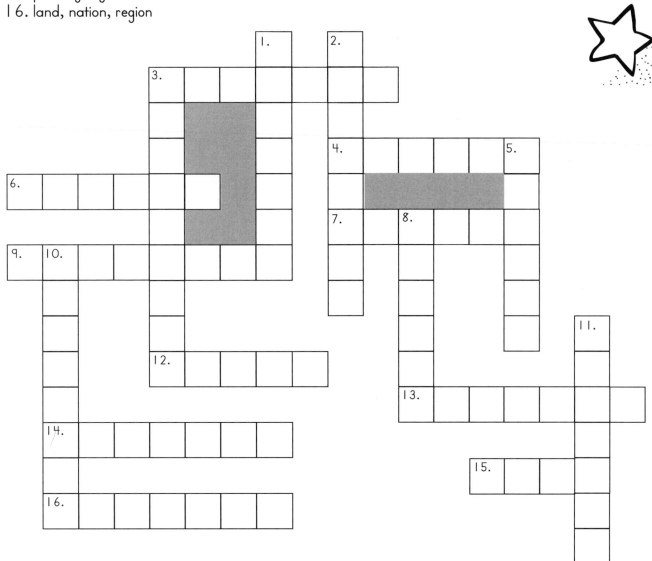

Name:	**Word Study**	

Phonics

Circle the sound for g.			Circle the sound for c.		
1. signal	g	j	1. country	s	k
2. energy	g	j	2. peaceful	s	k
3. bridge	g	j	3. since	s	k
4. figure	g	j	4. electric	s	k
5. dangerous	g	j	5. nice	s	k
6. regular	g	j	6. decided	s	k

Syllables

Divide these words into syllables.

1. country _____ _____

2. signal _____ _____

3. peaceful _____ _____

4. segment _____ _____

5. figure _____ _____

6. circle _____ _____

7. concert _____ _____

8. dancing _____ _____

9. genius _____ _____

10. dangerous _____ _____ _____

11. generous _____ _____ _____

12. electric _____ _____ _____

13. regular _____ _____ _____

14. decided _____ _____ _____

Name:

Edit for Spelling

Circle the words that are spelled correctly.

dancing	regular	desided
jenerous	sinse	figure
cirkle	danjerous	electric
signal	country	bridje
segment	energy	nise

Circle the misspelled words in the sentences. Write them correctly on the lines.

1. My family goes to the cuntry because it is so pieceful there.

   _____   _____

2. It was dangirous work building a brige over that canyon.

   _____   _____

3. Mr. Ruiz has been very genrous sinse he won the lottery.

   _____   _____

4. Everyone was dansing in a cirkle at the concirt.

   _____   _____   _____

Name:

Spelling List

18

Read and spell	Copy and spell	Spell and check
1. eagle		
2. example		
3. towel		
4. special		
5. legal		
6. little		
7. whole		
8. several		
9. terrible		
10. label		
11. question		
12. frequent		
13. telescope		
14. instead		
15. instrument		
16. celebrate		
17. declare		
18. address		
19. _____ (bonus word)		
20. _____ (bonus word)		

fold

Name:

Word Meaning

Fill in the blanks with words from Spelling List 18.

1. Harry had a _____ nightmare about a gigantic _____ that carried him away.

2. What musical _____ do you play?

3. Ann invited _____ friends over to help _____ her birthday.

4. _____ the _____ and place it on the package before you mail it.

5. My dad has a _____ _____ for studying the stars and planets.

6. Did they eat the _____ cake or only a _____ piece?

7. The teacher used my paper as an _____ of good handwriting.

Write sentences with these words.

[ ]

_____

_____

[ ]

_____

_____

Name:

Word Study

18

Phonics

| le | el | al |

Write the missing letters for the sound /l/ in these words.

1. eag_____
2. tow_____
3. speci_____
4. examp_____

5. leg_____
6. who_____
7. sever_____

8. lab_____
9. litt_____
10. terrib_____

Syllables

Match syllables to make words.
Write the complete words on the lines.

1. spe	quent	1. _special_
2. ques	dress	2. _____
3. fre	clare	3. _____
4. in	tion	4. _____
5. de	cial	5. _____
6. ad	stead	6. _____

1. ex	ri	ble	1. _example_
2. sev	e	al	2. _____
3. ter	e	ple	3. _____
4. cel	am	brate	4. _____
5. tel	stru	scope	5. _____
6. in	er	ment	6. _____

     Building Spelling Skills 5-6 EMC 727

Name: _____

Edit for Spelling

18

Circle the words that are spelled correctly.

exampel	special	labal
question	declair	address
twole	severul	freqwent
celebrate	telescope	leagle

Circle the misspelled words in the sentences. Write them correctly on the lines.

1. Sevral terible things happened to me yesterday.

   _____   _____

2. I saw an eegle in its nest through my teleskope.

   _____   _____

3. Mom bought a beach towle at a speshul sale.

   _____   _____

4. She had a qwestion about which insterment was needed for the operation.

   _____   _____

5. What is the uddress on the package's lable?

   _____   _____

Name:

Spelling List

19

Read and spell	Copy and spell	Spell and check
1. tried	_____	_____
2. weigh	_____	_____
3. piece	_____	_____
4. receive	_____	_____
5. their	_____	_____
6. fierce	_____	_____
7. neither	_____	_____
8. field	_____	_____
9. receiving	_____	_____
10. trying	_____	_____
11. hurried	_____	_____
12. siege	_____	_____
13. weighs	_____	_____
14. writing	_____	_____
15. tired	_____	_____
16. having	_____	_____
17. planned	_____	_____
18. worries	_____	_____
19. _____ (bonus word)	_____	_____
20. _____ (bonus word)	_____	_____

fold

Name: _____

Word Meaning

19

Complete the tasks using words from Spelling List 19.

1. Write the past tense form of these verbs.

a. try _____   c. tire _____

b. hurry _____   d. plan _____

2. Find the spelling word that is a pronoun. Use it in a sentence.

_____

3. Find the spelling words that are homophones for these words.

a. way _____

b. there _____

c. peace _____

4. Write the letter in front of the meaning for each word.

a. neither   _____ intense; savage

b. siege   _____ a piece of land used for crops or pasture

c. weigh   _____ one part of a whole thing

d. field   _____ not either

e. fierce   _____ measure how heavy something is

f. piece   _____ feels concern

g. worries   _____ surrounding a place for the purpose of capturing it

Building Spelling Skills

Name: _____

Phonics

Write the words in the correct boxes by vowel sounds.

Long a	Long e	Long i

tried   weigh   piece   field

receive   trying   siege

neither   writing   tired

Add Endings

Add an ending to the base word. Check how you changed the word.

add *ing*	no change	drop e; add ing	double final consonant
1. receive _____			
2. write _____			
3. plan _____			
4. worry _____			

add *ed*	no change	drop e; add ed	change y to i; add ed	double final consonant
1. receive _____				
2. worry _____				
3. plan _____				
4. try _____				

Name:

Edit for Spelling

19

Annie shared her great-grandmother's diary with her classmates. This entry was written during the drought on the Eastern Plains of Colorado in 1851.

**Circle the 11 misspelled words in this paragraph.
Write them correctly on the lines below.**

Dear Diary,

I'm tryin to help during this difficult time. The feerce winds are laying seige to the carefully planted feilds. We have seen neithur sun nor rain for seven days. The skies are like a piese of Granny's pewter. They're gray mood is hawving its effect on all of us.

Thomas worrys constantly, and Little Tom is so tarred of the blowing sand. Will it never end? I am writting this entry at dusk. As I put out the lantern tonight, I pray for a gentle rain to wet the soil and sun to warm the little plants and our spirits.

With a hopeful heart,
Viola

_____   _____   _____

_____   _____   _____

_____   _____   _____

_____   _____

Building Spelling Skills

Name:

Spelling List

20

Read and spell	Copy and spell	Spell and check
1. kindness		
2. darkness		
3. happiness		
4. loneliness		
5. sadness		
6. weakness		
7. exactly		
8. honestly		
9. speedily		
10. angrily		
11. happily		
12. friendly		
13. especially		
14. teacher		
15. actor		
16. liar		
17. biologist		
18. assistant		
19. _____ (bonus word)		
20. _____ (bonus word)		

fold

Building Spelling Skills 5-6 EMC 727

Name:

Word Meaning

Answer the questions using words from Spelling List 20.

1. What do you call someone who...?

    a. teaches   _____

    b. acts   _____

    c. tells lies   _____

    d. studies living things   _____

    e. helps others   _____

2. Which of these words describe how something might be done?

happiness   honestly   exactly

speedily   assistant   happily

3. Write the letter to match each word to its meaning.

    a. darkness   _____ specially

    b. loneliness   _____ in an angry manner

    c. especially   _____ absence of light

    d. angrily   _____ having no strength

    e. weakness   _____ a feeling of longing

Write sentences with these words.

	_____

_____

	_____

_____

                Building Spelling Skills 5-6 EMC 727

Name:

Word Study

20

Suffixes

Add the suffix to each word.

ness	
1. dark	_____
2. lonely	_____
3. weak	_____
4. happy	_____

ly	
1. honest	_____
2. angry	_____
3. friend	_____
4. speedy	_____

Now circle the words that required a change before adding the suffix.

Base Words

Write the base word and suffix.

	base word	suffix
1. sadness	sad	ness
2. teacher	_____	_____
3. happily	_____	_____
4. kindness	_____	_____
5. exactly	_____	_____
6. liar	_____	_____
7. loneliness	_____	_____
8. actor	_____	_____

       Building Spelling Skills 5-6 EMC 727

Name: _____

Edit for Spelling

Circle the words that are spelled correctly.

lonelyness	biologist	lier	honestly	speedily
kindness	teacher	sadness	happiness	assisstant
exactly	weekness	darkness	espeshully	freindly

Circle the misspelled words in the sentences. Write them correctly on the lines.

1. That lyer never answered honistly.

   _____   _____

2. His new teecher was frindly to the new students.

   _____   _____

3. The biologest's assistent worked speedyly.

   _____   _____   _____

4. An acter must know exacly what to do when the stage is plunged into darknes.

   _____   _____   _____

Building Spelling Skills

Name: _____

Spelling List

21

Read and spell	Copy and spell	Spell and check
1. scene	_____	_____
2. they're	_____	_____
3. through	_____	_____
4. heir	_____	_____
5. clothes	_____	_____
6. byte	_____	_____
7. aloud	_____	_____
8. cruise	_____	_____
9. crews	_____	_____
10. isle	_____	_____
11. principal	_____	_____
12. principle	_____	_____
13. hour	_____	_____
14. knew	_____	_____
15. two	_____	_____
16. write	_____	_____
17. chute	_____	_____
18. reign	_____	_____
19. _____ (bonus word)	_____	_____
20. _____ (bonus word)	_____	_____

fold

Name:

Word Meaning

21

Complete the crossword puzzle using words from Spelling List 21.

**(There are two words in this puzzle that are not on your spelling list.
See if you can figure them out.)**

Across

1. a group of computer bits
4. the head of a school
10. the period of time a king rules the country
11. a person that inherits the property of another person
12. an abbreviation for submarine
14. the place where an event or action occurs
16. thoughts expressed vocally are said
17. contraction for they are
18. a small island

Down

2. in one end of a tunnel and out at the other end
3. garments to wear on the body
5. a steep slide
6. a basic truth or law
7. a period of time
8. sail about from place to place
9. to record thoughts in written form
13. something that makes a ringing sound
15. groups of people working together

Building Spelling Skills 5-6 EMC 727

Name: _____

Word Study

21

Homophones

Use the words on Spelling List 21 to write the homophones for these words.

1. seen _____
2. rain _____
3. threw _____
4. their _____
5. crews _____
6. principle _____
7. right _____
8. air _____

9. allowed _____
10. our _____
11. too _____
12. bite _____
13. I'll _____
14. close _____
15. new _____
16. shoot _____

Phonics

Write these words in the correct boxes.

long e	long a	long i

long o	ow as in now	oo as in too

they're	scene	aloud	byte	through	clothes
reign	isle	cruise	hour	write	knew
seen	close	☆			

Building Spelling Skills 5-6 EMC 727

Name:

Edit for Spelling

21

Circle the 10 misspelled words below. Write them correctly on the lines.

Imagine this seen –– the princepal in freshly pressed close running threw a fountain of tomato juice. It all happened an our before lunch yesterday.

The kitchen had been closed so that too cruise of electricians could replace some wiring in the cafeteria. Mr. Grant, the principal, was on his way to check their work. Just as he entered the kitchen, the electric can opener buzzed into action. A huge can of tomato juice that had been left on the can opener became the victim of Newton's principel of action and reaction. The can opener went down, the can was opened, and just as the principal walked in, it flew off the countertop, drenching him in juice.

Much mopping and ten damp towels later, Mr. Grant was ready to walk back to his office. And what about the electricians? Their working on a crews ship heading toward Alaska. I wonder if the ship has a can opener?

_____   _____

_____   _____

_____   _____

_____   _____

_____   _____

Name:

Spelling List

22

Read and spell	Copy and spell	Spell and check
1. thoughtful		
2. successful		
3. wasteful		
4. wonderful		
5. skillful		
6. plentiful		
7. government		
8. amusement		
9. predicament		
10. excitement		
11. punishment		
12. arrangement		
13. fearless		
14. careless		
15. worthless		
16. thoughtless		
17. useless		
18. reckless		
19. _____ (bonus word)		
20. _____ (bonus word)		

fold

Word Meaning

22

Match each spelling word to its meaning.

b 1. careless

___ 2. arrangement

___ 3. excitement

___ 4. amusement

___ 5. fearless

___ 6. predicament

___ 7. reckless

___ 8. punishment

___ 9. successful

___ 10. worthless

___ 11. thoughtful

___ 12. wonderful

___ 13. government

___ 14. wasteful

a. entertainment

b. not paying enough attention

c. afraid of nothing

d. the way in which things are organized

e. an excited condition

f. an unpleasant or difficult situation

g. being punished

h. rash or careless

i. good for nothing

j. ending in success

k. considerate

l. marvelous

m. the ruling of a country, state, or city

n. using or spending too much

Write sentences with these words.

Building Spelling Skills

Name: _____

Suffixes

Add the correct suffix to the base word.

ful	– full of
ment	– quality or state of
less	– without

1. The builder's _____ work caused the building to collapse.
   (care)

2. There will be great_____ when the ship lands on Mars.
   (excite)

3. Her_____ behavior made her a popular nurse.
   (thought)

4. That flat ball will be _____ in the basketball game.
   (use)

5. What kind of _____ does Egypt have?
   (govern)

6. Food was _____ at the company picnic.
   (plenty)

Syllables

Divide these words into syllables. Then circle the suffix.

reckless   reck (less)

1. careless   _____ _____

2. wasteful   _____ _____

3. thoughtless   _____ _____

4. plentiful   _____ _____ _____

5. amusement   _____ _____ _____

6. wonderful   _____ _____ _____

7. excitement   _____ _____ _____

8. successful   _____ _____ _____

Circle the words with the correct suffix.

thoughtment	arrangeful	careless
punishful	thoughtless	worthment
reckless	arrangement	carely
reckful	fearment	excitement
worthless	useful	

Circle the misspelled words in the sentences. Write them correctly on the lines.

1. It is usless to worry about that carless mistake.

   _____   _____

2. Our arranjment was to meet at the amusment park at 9 o'clock.

   _____   _____

3. Do you think his wreckless behavior deserved such a harsh punichment?

   _____   _____

4. The goverment was finally sucessful in reaching a peeceful solution

   to the disagreement.

   _____   _____   _____

Name:

Spelling List

23

Read and spell	Copy and spell	Spell and check
1. shoes		
2. sure		
3. sugar		
4. musician		
5. patience		
6. mission		
7. occasion		
8. physician		
9. tension		
10. conclusion		
11. constitution		
12. caution		
13. constellation		
14. addition		
15. fiction		
16. position		
17. official		
18. glacier		
19. _____ (bonus word)		
20. _____ (bonus word)		

fold

Name:

Word Meaning

23

Complete the crossword puzzle using words from Spelling List 23.
(There are two words in this puzzle that are not on your spelling list. See if you can figure them out.)

Across

1. urge to be careful
4. person holding a public office
6. the end
8. a sweet substance
12. group of stars
13. a mathematical process where sets are combined
14. a metal container for food
15. coverings for people's feet
16. a large mass of very slowly moving ice

Down

2. the opposite of yes
3. something made up
5. the principles by which a country is governed
7. a person who plays music
9. a doctor
10. the act of waiting without complaining
11. stress or strain
15. without any doubt

Name:

Word Study

Phonics

Circle the letters in each word that have the sound of /sh/.

1. shoes
2. glacier
3. caution
4. sure

5. official
6. addition
7. sugar
8. position

How many different ways was the /sh/ sound spelled? _____

Syllables

Match the syllables to make spelling words. Write the complete words on the lines.

1. fic   ar   1. _____
2. sug   sion   2. _____
3. pa   tion   3. _____
4. mis   cier   4. _____
5. gla   tience   5. _____

1. phy   clu   cial   1. _____
2. con   fi   tion   2. _____
3. of   di   sion   3. _____
4. ad   si   cian   4. _____

Building Spelling Skills

Name: _____

Edit for Spelling

Circle the words that are spelled correctly.

shoes	shure	caution	glacier
fiktion	suger	poisician	musician
mision	official	ocassion	tension

Circle the misspelled words in the sentences. Write them correctly on the lines.

1. Be shure to tie your shoos.

   _____   _____

2. His missun was to study glasher movements.

   _____   _____

3. It takes pacience to become a great musition.

   _____   _____

4. The fysician plays tennis to relieve tenshun.

   _____   _____

5. What was the conclushun of the ficshun story?

   _____   _____

6. His oficial posssion is city councilman.

   _____   _____

Name:

Spelling List

24

Read and spell	**Copy and spell**	**Spell and check**
1. wrestle		
2. wrong		
3. answer		
4. dough		
5. unknown		
6. knapsack		
7. often		
8. listen		
9. climb		
10. half		
11. island		
12. talking		
13. design		
14. scratch		
15. tonight		
16. limb		
17. knot		
18. whistle		
19. _____ (bonus word)		
20. _____ (bonus word)		

fold

Building Spelling Skills

Name: _____

Word Meaning

Answer these questions using the words on Spelling List 24.

1. Which spelling words are the opposites of these words?

a. right _____

b. ask _____

c. seldom _____

d. speak _____

2. Which spelling words are compound words?

a. _____   b. _____

3. Which spelling words mean about the same as these words?

a. incorrect _____

b. respond _____

c. frequently _____

d. hear _____

4. Add a prefix to make this word mean "not known."

_____known

5. Which word means.....?

a. something you make cookies from _____

b. a piece of land surrounded by water _____

c. a part of the whole thing _____

d. make a sound by blowing through your lips _____

Write sentences with these words.

[_____] _____

_____

[_____] _____

_____

Building Spelling Skills

Name:

Phonics

Which of the bold letters are silent? Circle them.

1. w(re)st(le)
2. answer
3. often

4. climb
5. talking
6. knot

7. half
8. whistle
9. tonight

10. island
11. design
12. scratch

Fill in the missing letters.

| wr | kn | mb | lf |

1. _____ong
2. un_____own

3. li_____en
4. li_____

5. _____apsack
6. _____ite

7. bo_____
8. ca_____

Phonics

What type of vowel sounds do the underlined letters represent?

	short vowel	long vowel	schwa
1. wrestle	X		
2. often			
3. climb			
4. listen			
5. half			
6. answer			
7. dough			
8. knapsack			
9. island			

Name:

Edit for Spelling

24

Circle the 13 misspelled words below. Write them correctly on the lines.

This summer I went camping on an islend near my home. I carried everything I would need in a napsack. When I reached the ranger station, he was talkin about which campsites were still available for camping tonite. I asked about a campsite near the lake. His anser was to nod his head and point to a trail going up to the left.

I climmed down a slope to the lake. I found a level spot to set up camp. I hung my supplies on a tree limm using a special not my scout leader had taught me. I pitched my tent, prepared doe for biscuits, and started a fire.

While I waited for the griddle to get hot, I sat on a log and tried to scrach a desine on a chunk of wood. What a peaceful way to spend an afternoon. Then everything started to go wrawng. The sky opened up and rain slammed down to the ground! I crawled into the tent quickly, but I looked like I had restled a bear in a mud puddle. I hoped the downpour would be over soon. I was hungry for those biscuits!

_____   _____   _____

_____   _____   _____

_____   _____   _____

_____

Building Spelling Skills

Name: _____

Spelling List

25

Read and spell	Copy and spell	Spell and check
1. rewrite	_____	_____
2. reappear	_____	_____
3. recall	_____	_____
4. recover	_____	_____
5. rebuild	_____	_____
6. dishonest	_____	_____
7. disagree	_____	_____
8. disappear	_____	_____
9. disappoint	_____	_____
10. disconnect	_____	_____
11. disapprove	_____	_____
12. misbehave	_____	_____
13. misfortune	_____	_____
14. misunderstand	_____	_____
15. misspell	_____	_____
16. misuse	_____	_____
17. illegal	_____	_____
18. illegible	_____	_____
19. _____ (bonus word)	_____	_____
20. _____ (bonus word)	_____	_____

fold

Name:

Word Meaning

⭐ 25

Complete these tasks using words from Spelling List 25.

1. Write the spelling word that means...

a. not neat enough to read _____

b. spell incorrectly _____

c. fail to satisfy a wish or need _____

d. build something again _____

e. bad luck _____

f. use something incorrectly _____

2. Read the word. Then write the meaning for its prefix.

a. rewrite − **re** means _____

b. disagree − **dis** means _____

c. misbehave − **mis** means _____

d. illegal − **il** means _____

Write sentences with these words.

_____ _____

_____

_____ _____

_____

Building Spelling Skills

Name:

Word Study

Root Words

Add the correct prefix to the base word.

dis	re	mis	il

1. Dad did not wish to _____ the children, so he rushed to
   (appoint)
   get to the game on time.

2. We promised Mother we wouldn't _____ at the restaurant.
   (behave)

3. Many people had to _____ their homes after the hurricane.
   (build)

4. It is _____ to drive a car without a license.
   (legal)

5. Did you _____ the directions for last night's homework?
   (understand)

6. My allowance seems to_____ as soon as I get it!
   (appear)

Add a prefix to make each word into its opposite.

1. honest _____dishonest_____   4. approve _____

2. agree _____   5. legible _____

3. legal _____   6. connect _____

Name:

Edit for Spelling

25

Circle the words with a correct prefix.

recover   dislegible   misappear   disappoint

disfortune   rebehave   illegal   illegible

ilbuild   disfortune   dishonest   ilspell

reunderstand   recall

Circle the misspelled words in the sentences. Write them correctly on the lines.

1. The town had to rebiuld both homes and businesses after the
   terrible misfortunate brought on by the tornado.

   _____   _____

2. Do you rekall how to disconect the VCR?

   _____   _____

3. The minister will desapprove if we missbehave in church.

   _____   _____

4. If you mispell words and use ilegible handwriting, you will have
   to reright your story.

   _____   _____   _____

Building Spelling Skills

Name: _____

Spelling List

Read and spell	Copy and spell	Spell and check
1. paragraph	_____	_____
2. trophy	_____	_____
3. nephew	_____	_____
4. enough	_____	_____
5. cough	_____	_____
6. fourth	_____	_____
7. Friday	_____	_____
8. physical	_____	_____
9. roughest	_____	_____
10. pharmacy	_____	_____
11. fragile	_____	_____
12. fluid	_____	_____
13. briefly	_____	_____
14. festival	_____	_____
15. stuffed	_____	_____
16. triumph	_____	_____
17. telephone	_____	_____
18. few	_____	_____
19. _____ (bonus word)	_____	_____
20. _____ (bonus word)	_____	_____

fold

Building Spelling Skills 5-6 EMC 727

Name:

Word Meaning

26

Complete the crossword puzzle using words from Spelling List 26.

Across

2. a group of sentences about the same idea
5. an instrument for talking between two distant points
8. not many
10. a drugstore
11. force air from your lungs with a sudden effort and noise
12. success or victory
13. in a short manner

Down

1. the son of your brother or sister
3. pertaining to the body
4. a celebration
6. as much as is needed
7. an award often in the form of a statue or cup
8. easily broken
9. an ordinal number

Building Spelling Skills

Name: _____

Word Study

Phonics

| f | ph | gh |

Fill in the letters that stand for the sound /f/.

1. paragra_____
2. _____ew
3. tro_____y
4. tele_____one
5. enou_____
6. ne_____ew
7. brie_____ly
8. rou_____est
9. _____armacy
10. _____estival
11. cou_____
12. stuf_____ed
13. _____luid
14. _____ysical
15. _____ragile
16. trium_____

Synonyms

Write the spelling word that means about the same as these words.

1. award   _____
2. plenty   _____
3. drugstore   _____
4. liquid   _____
5. delicate   _____
6. handful   _____
7. victory   _____
8. shortly   _____

Write the correct synonyms to complete the sentences.

1. She received a _____ after her great _____.
   (award)   (victory)

2. Mrs. Chan bought a _____ teacup from the _____.
   (delicate)   (drugstore)

3. The host spoke _____ after the guests had eaten _____.
   (shortly)   (plenty)

Name:

Edit for Spelling

26

Circle the 11 misspelled words below. Write them correctly on the lines.

From my bed I saw the trophee sitting on my desk. I smiled. It had been a triumf followed by a disaster. It all happened last friday. I went with my neffew to the Obon Festtival. We were to compete in a Kendo competition. The crowd that had gathered loved those phisical duels.

In traditional dress the competitors moved like frajle dancers around the ring. Breefly lunging toward each other and then stepping back, the competitors performed. It was one of the ruffest contests we had entered, and we were lucky enuf to win.

As the trophy was presented, we bowed and stepped from the stage. I tripped on the forth step and fell -- triumph followed by disaster. The graceful warrior is now grounded with a broken ankle!

_____   _____   _____

_____   _____   _____

_____   _____   _____

_____   _____

 Building Spelling Skills 5-6 EMC 727

Name:

Spelling List

27

Read and spell	Copy and spell	Spell and check
1. imperfect		
2. impolite		
3. impatient		
4. improper		
5. inactive		
6. inconvenient		
7. incorrect		
8. inconsiderate		
9. preview		
10. prejudice		
11. prevent		
12. prefix		
13. prehistoric		
14. unable		
15. uncertain		
16. uncomfortable		
17. unaware		
18. ungrateful		
19. _____ (bonus word)		
20. _____ (bonus word)		

fold

| Name: | **Word Meaning**  |

Fill in the blanks with words from Spelling List 27.

1. A small crack made the cup _____ .

2. It is _____ to always take the largest piece.

3. Bears are _____ during the cold winter months.

4. Our teacher was _____ when she was _____ to keep the class on task.

5. He was _____ that his _____ behavior made other people feel _____ .

6. Prof. Singh will _____ that new book about _____ animals before using it in his class.

7. I dialed an _____ telephone _____, so I couldn't complete my long-distance call.

8. How can we _____ _____ against others from happening?

Write sentences with these words.

```
[          ] _____

_____

[          ] _____

_____
```

Name:

Word Study

27

Root Words

Add the correct prefix to each base word.

1. not perfect   _____perfect

2. judgement without knowledge   _____judice

3. contains mistakes   _____correct

4. not sure   _____certain

5. inspect beforehand   _____view

6. keep from happening   _____vent

7. causing difficulty   _____convenient

8. put before a word to change its meaning   _____fix

9. not conscious   _____aware

10. lacking good manners   _____polite

Antonyms

Write the spelling word that is an antonym for each word.

1. perfect _____

2. polite _____

3. aware _____

4. active _____

5. grateful _____

6. patient _____

7. considerate _____

8. historic _____

9. comfortable _____

10. convenient _____

11. able _____

12. proper _____

Circle the words with the correct prefix.

inpolite	uncorrect	prevent
unaware	inconsiderate	unview
prehistoric	unproper	uncertain
preactive	inconvenient	inable
unpatient	imperfect	ingrateful
prejudice	incomfortable	prefix

Circle the misspelled words in the sentences. Write them on the lines below.

1. The words impolight and inkonsiderate have about the same meaning.

   _____   _____

2. We went to a prevue showing of a new movie about life in perhistoric times.

   _____   _____

3. The test made him uncomterble because he was unsertain about how to do the math problems.

   _____   _____

4. I was unawear that my telephone perfix had been changed from 408 to 412.

   _____   _____

Name:

Spelling List

28

Read and spell	Copy and spell	Spell and check
1. geology		
2. geometry		
3. geography		
4. geologist		
5. action		
6. enact		
7. transport		
8. import		
9. portable		
10. bicycle		
11. cyclone		
12. encyclopedia		
13. autograph		
14. automobile		
15. automatic		
16. autobiography		
17. telegraph		
18. photograph		
19. _____ (bonus word)		
20. _____ (bonus word)		

fold

Name:

Word Meaning

28

Complete the crossword puzzle using words from Spelling List 28.

Across

1. a person who is an expert in geology
4. a two-wheeled vehicle moved by pushing pedals
6. a violent windstorm
9. self-written story of your life
12. a passenger vehicle powered by an engine
13. device for sending coded messages over wires
14. make into law

Down

2. study of the earth's surface, climate, and people
3. carry from one place to another
5. a set of books giving information
7. easily carried
8. something being done
10. a picture made with a camera
11. to bring something in from another country

Building Spelling Skills

Root Words

Use the words in the boxes to help you answer the questions.

root words		prefixes	suffixes
geo – earth	**cycle** – circle	**auto** – self	**ology** – study of
act – do	**photo** – light	**trans** – across	**ist** – one who studies
bio – life	**graph** – write	**bi** – two	**tion** – state of being
port – carry			**ile** – state of being

What word parts make words meaning...?

1. "the study of the earth"

   __geo__ + __ology__ = __geology__
   root   suffix

2. "writing of the story of yourself"

   _____ + _____ + _____ = _____
   prefix   root   root

3. "carry something across a distance"

   _____ + _____ = _____
   prefix   root

4. "record using light"

   _____ + _____ = _____
   root   root

5. "doing something"

   _____ + _____ = _____
   root   suffix

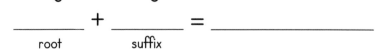

Name:

Edit for Spelling

28

Circle the 10 misspelled words below. Write them correctly on the lines.

Frank is better than an automatick encylopydia. If you ask him about anything, he always has the answer. I needed help finding Malaysia. No problem – – Frank is good at geogruphy. My dad's car sounded strange. No problem –– Frank understands automobeles. He helped my sister with her geomtrie, my mother with geollogy, and my grandfather with his autobiografy. No problem! Frank is my own special portabel library. He helps me emport and transprot information. Frank is what I named my new computer!

_____   _____

_____   _____

_____   _____

_____   _____

_____   _____

Name:

Spelling List

29

Read and spell	Copy and spell	Spell and check
1. destruct		
2. destruction		
3. describe		
4. description		
5. decorate		
6. decoration		
7. divide		
8. division		
9. administer		
10. administration		
11. populate		
12. population		
13. infect		
14. infection		
15. punctuate		
16. punctuation		
17. attend		
18. attention		
19. _____ (bonus word)		
20. _____ (bonus word)		

fold

Building Spelling Skills 5-6 EMC 727

Name:

Word Meaning

29

Fill in the blanks with words from Spelling List 29.

1. Aunt Jill is going to _____ my birthday cake.
   She always makes a beautiful _____.

2. Be sure to_____ your story correctly.
   I am going to check your _____ skills.

3. Plans to _____ the old building have been approved.
   Carefully placed explosives will cause its_____ .

4. Who was hired to_____ that special project?
   The college _____ hired three people to do the job.

5. In the 1800s people were encouraged to _____ the
   western territories. Today many western cities have a large
   _____ .

6. If you keep picking at that sore, you may _____ it.
   And _____ will make it more difficult to heal.

7. Did you _____ the science lecture?
   I paid close_____ so I'd be sure to understand.

Building Spelling Skills 5-6 EMC 727

Name:

Word Study

29

Suffix–tion

Add the suffix tion **to change these verbs to nouns. Some spelling changes will be needed.**

1. destruct _____

2. infect _____

3. attend _____

4. describe _____

5. decorate _____

6. administer _____

7. populate _____

8. divide _____

9. punctuate _____

Syllables

Divide these words into syllables.

1. destruct _____ _____

2. divide _____ _____

3. description _____ _____ _____

4. decorate _____ _____ _____

5. infection _____ _____ _____

6. populate _____ _____ _____

7. punctuate _____ _____ _____

8. attention _____ _____ _____

9. administer _____ _____ _____ _____

10. decoration _____ _____ _____ _____

11. punctuation _____ _____ _____ _____

| Name: | # Edit for Spelling |  29 |

Circle the words that are spelled correctly.

disstruction	description	decorate
populat	puntuashun	attention
admenister	infection	administration
dekoration	divizion	enfect
uttend	describe	population
punctuate	devide	destruct

Circle the misspelled words in the sentences. Write them correctly on the lines below.

1. Can you discribe the decorashun on the banner?

   _____   _____

2. The owner plans to devide the admenestration of his company into three departments.

   _____   _____

3. Pay atention as you write your story so that the spelling and puntuation are correct.

   _____   _____

4. Ten percent of the populacian was infectted with smallpox.

   _____   _____

Building Spelling Skills

Name: _____

Spelling List

Read and spell	Copy and spell	Spell and check
1. multiply	_____	_____
2. temperature	_____	_____
3. vertical	_____	_____
4. equation	_____	_____
5. currency	_____	_____
6. amphibian	_____	_____
7. intersection	_____	_____
8. environment	_____	_____
9. agriculture	_____	_____
10. frequency	_____	_____
11. civilization	_____	_____
12. manufacture	_____	_____
13. characteristic	_____	_____
14. atmosphere	_____	_____
15. representative	_____	_____
16. semicircle	_____	_____
17. substitute	_____	_____
18. technology	_____	_____
19. _____ (bonus word)	_____	_____
20. _____ (bonus word)	_____	_____

fold

Building Spelling Skills 5-6 EMC 727

Name: _____

Word Meaning

Complete this task using words from Spelling List 30.

Write the spelling word that means...

1. straight up and down _____

2. a member of a group of cold-blooded animals with moist skin and a backbone _____

3. place where one thing crosses another _____

4. the raising of crops and farm animals _____

5. rate at which something happens _____

6. half a circle _____

7. the money used in a country _____

8. the gases surrounding the earth _____

9. the culture of a people or period of time _____

10. something used in place of another thing _____

11. a mathematical statement that two quantities are equal _____

12. a measurement of the degree of heat or cold _____

Write sentences with these words.

[_____] _____

_____

[_____] _____

Name:

Word Study

30

Syllables

Fill in the missing syllables.

1. mul_____ply
2. verti_____
3. e_____tion
4. _____rency
5. fre_____cy
6. atmos_____

7. _____stitute
8. _____acter_____tic
9. repre_____a_____
10. _____icir_____
11. _____nology
12. tempera_____

13. am_____ian
14. in_____sec_____
15. en_____ron_____
16. agri_____ture
17. _____iliza_____
18. man_____ _____tu

Count Syllables

Count the number of syllables in these words. Write the words in the correct boxes.

3 syllables	4 syllables	5 syllables

temperature   vertical   amphibian

intersection   equation   environment

agriculture   civilization   multiply

manufacture   characteristic   atmosphere

semicircle   technology   representative

substitute   currency   frequency

Name:

Edit for Spelling

30

Circle the misspelled words in the sentences. Write them correctly on the lines.

1. Can an amfibian live in an envirunment where the temperachur is very low?

   _____   _____   _____

2. The math equasion required me to mulltiply fractions.

   _____   _____

3. That prehistoric civilisation had advanced to a stage where agrikulture was important.

   _____   _____

4. What kind of atmusphere is characturistic of Venus?

   _____   _____

5. The government representuteves stood in a semycircle around the new monument.

   _____   _____

6. You will need to substutute English pounds for your American kurrency when you visit Great Britain.

   _____   _____

7. His company will manufacter stop signs to place at the intersecton of Main Street and Fifth Avenue.

   _____   _____

Spelling Checklist

Spelling List Number	Student Names													
1														
2														
3														
4														
5														
6														
7														
8														
9														
10														
11														
12														
13														
14														
15														
16														
17														
18														
19														
20														
21														
22														
23														
24														
25														
26														
27														
28														
29														
30														

Individual Spelling Record

Date	Spelling List	Number Correct	Words Missed	Comments

Name:

Spelling

1. _____
2. _____
3. _____
4. _____
5. _____
6. _____
7. _____
8. _____
9. _____
10. _____

11. _____
12. _____
13. _____
14. _____
15. _____
16. _____
17. _____
18. _____
19. _____
20. _____

☆ Review Words

1. _____   2. _____   3. _____

Sentence Dictation

1. _____

_____

2. _____

_____

3. _____

_____

Name:

Spelling List

Read and spell	Copy and spell	Spell and check
1.	_____	_____
2.	_____	_____
3.	_____	_____
4.	_____	_____
5.	_____	_____
6.	_____	_____
7.	_____	_____
8.	_____	_____
9.	_____	_____
10.	_____	_____
11.	_____	_____
12.	_____	_____
13.	_____	_____
14.	_____	_____
15.	_____	_____
16.	_____	_____
17.	_____	_____
18.	_____	_____
19. _____ (bonus word)	_____	_____
20. _____ (bonus word)	_____	_____

fold

Building Spelling Skills

Note: Reproduce this page to make your own crossword puzzles.

Name:

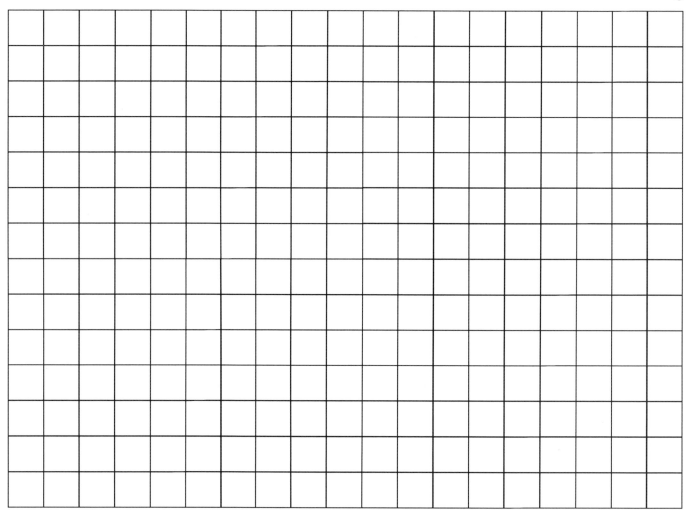

Across	Down

Name:

Word Sort

Read the words.
Write them in the boxes.

Note: Reproduce this letter to send home with spelling lists.

Dear Parents,

Attached is your child's spelling list for this week. Encourage him/her to practice the words in one or more of these ways.

1. Read and spell each word. Cover it up and write it. Uncover the word and check to see if it is correct.

2. Find the words on the spelling list in printed materials such as books and magazines.

3. You read a word aloud and ask your child to spell it (either aloud or written on paper).

Thank you for your support of our spelling program.

Sincerely,

Dear Parents,

Attached is your child's spelling list for this week. Encourage him/her to practice the words in one or more of these ways.

1. Read and spell each word. Cover it up and write it. Uncover the word and check to see if it is correct.

2. Find the words on the spelling list in printed materials such as books and magazines.

3. You read a word aloud and ask your child to spell it (either aloud or written on paper).

Thank you for your support of our spelling program.

Sincerely,

Answer Key

Page 25
1. oxygen   until
2. cousin   grudge   umpire
3. thumb   stunt
4. another   city
5. sudden   began   very
6. copy   trouble

Sentences will vary.

Page 26
rough   thumb   trouble
grudge   once   cousin
stunt   another   until
sudden   does   umpire

1. began   5. umpire
2. opposite   6. which
3. another   7. city
4. copy   8. until

1. trou—til   1. trouble
2. cous—gan   2. cousin
3. be—ble   3. began
4. cop—y   4. copy
5. un—den   5. until
6. um—in   6. umpire
7. sud—y   7. sudden
8. cit—pire   8. city

Page 27
These words should be circled.
1. grudge   7. umpire
2. another   8. city
3. does   9. until
4. trouble   10. which
5. cousin   11. thumb
6. oxygen   12. very

These words should be circled and written correctly.
1. cuzin   unother   sity
   cousin   another   city
2. oxigin   entil   begun
   oxygen   until   began
3. Wunce   truble   stunts
   Once   trouble   stunt
4. Duz   verie   ruff
   Does   very   rough

Page 29
across   down
1. radio   2. April
5. payment   3. favorite
7. relation   4. straight
8. sleigh   6. explain
10. afraid   7. raise
11. freight   9. height
13. station   12. trace
14. daybreak   15. able
16. laid

Page 30
1. payment   10. radio
2. raise   11. daybreak
3. they   12. explain
4. able   13. laid
5. relation   14. April
6. afraid   15. trace
7. sleigh   16. freight
8. straight   17. station
9. favorite

no long a - height

These words should be underlined and marked.
April   station
able   relation
radio   favorite

Page 31
These words should be circled.
1. payment   7. favorite
2. height   8. April
3. afraid   9. radio
4. relation   10. explain
5. daybreak   11. straight
6. laid   12. raise

These words should be circled and written correctly.
1. Aprul   faverute
   April   favorite
2. paiment   slay
   payment   sleigh
3. explane   radeo
   explain   radio
4. layed   straite   frayt
   laid   straight   freight

Page 33
1. fifteen eager (or ready) referee
2. Please cube unusual
   (or beautiful) (or cute)
3. fuel ready universe
4. easily (or maybe) beautiful
   (or unusual)
5. communicate ecology future
Sentences will vary.

Page 34
long e   long u
fifteen   cube
eager   universe
referee   future
easily   communicate
ready   fuel
please   cute
maybe   unusual
only
ecology

1. 3   4. 4   7. 3   10. 3
2. 3   5. 1   8. 4   11. 2
3. 2   6. 4   9. 1   12. 2

Page 35
These words should be circled.
1. eager   7. fuel
2. ready   8. easily
3. cute   9. future
4. been   10. maybe
5. please   11. fifteen
6. beautiful   12. cube

These words should be circled and written correctly.
1. Plez   fiftene   reddy
   Please   fifteen   ready
2. refree   cummunikate   ownlee
   referee   communicate   only
3. eegir   unuzual   kube
   eager   unusual   cube
4. bin   fewl
   been   fuel

Page 37
1. a. awoke   d. obey
   b. throat   e. goal
   c. oldest   f. owner

2. b   c
   f   g
   a   d
   e

3. a. obey   e. awoke
  b. hello   f. followed
  c. approach g. broken
  d. oldest

Sentences will vary.

Page 38

obey   program
poem   tomorrow
hello   broken
wrote   potato
goal   throat
ocean   oldest
approach   spoken
owner   awoke

1. past   7. present
2. present/past 8. past
3. present   9. present
4. past   10. past
5. past   11. present
6. present/past 12. present

Page 39

These words should be circled.
1. obey   7. goal
2. ocean   8. potato
3. poem   9. tomorrow
4. owner   10. program
5. approach 11. throat
6. wrote   12. awoke

These words should be circled
and written correctly.
1. gole   oshun   tomorro
   goal   ocean   tomorrow
2. oldist obay
   oldest obey
3. borken putato throte
   broken potato throat
4. onner   rote   pome
   owner   wrote poem

Page 41

1. a. of the clock   i. we are
  b. I have   j. it is
  c. will not   k. did not
  d. I will   l. are not

e. they have   m. you are
f. does not   n. who is
g. do not   o. have not
h. there is   p. could not

2. a. it's
  b. couldn't didn't
  c. don't   aren't
  d. Who's   o'clock

Sentences will vary.

Page 42

1. I'll   w i
2. haven't   o
3. we're   a
4. they've   h a
5. couldn't   o
6. you're   a
7. there's   i
8. doesn't   o
9. it's   i
10. I've   h a
11. who's   i
12. don't   o

1. they're   5. wasn't
2. we'll   6. they'll
3. wouldn't   7. hasn't
4. she's   8. he's

who's, whose, who's

Page 43

1. I'll   6. it's
2. won't   7. didn't
3. o'clock   8. aren't
4. doesn't   9. you're
5. there's   10. haven't

These words should be circled
and written correctly.
1. Culdn't   couldn't
2. Who's   Whose
3. Ive'   they'r.e
   I've   they're
4. Theyv'e   do'nt
   They've   don't
5. Were   Wo'nt
   We're   Won't
6. Ill   whose
   I'll   who's

Page 45

Across	Down
2. smiling	1. silent
3. license	4. inquire
6. knight	5. quite
9. idea	7. higher
11. rhyme	8. variety
12. widest	10. lying
13. diagram	
14. python	

Page 46

1. lying   10. smiling
2. idea   11. knight
3. silent   12. quite
4. python   13. variety
5. widest   14. I'm
6. rhyme   15. buy
7. myself   16. higher
8. apply   17. license
9. diagram   18. inquire

1. lying - change ie to y and
  add ing
2. smiled - drop the final e and
  add ed
3. inquired - drop the e and add
  ed (As this rule is confusing
  to some students, you may
  choose to accept "add d" in 2
  and 3.)
4. buying - just add ing

Page 47

These words should be circled.
2. rhyme   11. myself
5. python 12. idea
8. lying   14. diagram

These words should be circled
and written correctly.
1. knite   diagarm
   knight   diagram
2. miself   smileng silunt
   myself   smiling silent
3. pyton   hier
   python   higher
4. Im   bye   varitee
   I'm   buy   variety

Page 49
1. a. could (should)   d. duty
   b. school   e. rookie
   c. threw (clue)   f. truth

2. a. gloomy   f. choose
   b. threw   g. clue
   c. rookie   h. truth
   d. understood   i. bulletin
   e. route   j. ruin

Sentences will vary.

Page 50

/u/ - look	/ü/ - too
understood	gloomy
neighborhood	school
rookie	loose
could	choose
should	route
bulletin	clue
	truth
	duty
	threw
	ruin
	Tuesday
	usually

1. gloom — ie   1. gloomy
2. rook — in   2. rookie
3. du — y   3. duty
4. ru — day   4. ruin
5. Tues — ty   5. Tuesday

Page 51
These words should be circled.
2. school   11. bulletin
4. rookie   14. usually
6. truth   15. ruin

These words should be circled
and written correctly.
1. gloome   rooin
   gloomy   ruin
2. klew   trooth
   clue   truth

3. nayberhood   usully   skool
   neighborhood usually school
4. undrestood   bulliten
   understood   bulletin

Page 53
1. Moisture   mountain
2. oyster   spoil
3. ounce   amount
4. allow   annoy
5. royal   employ
6. sprout   boundary   house

Sentences will vary.

Page 54
1. choice   1. ground
2. royal   2. house
3. spoil   3. boundary
4. avoid   4. allow
5. employ   5. mountain
6. moisture   6. ourselves
7. oyster   7. somehow
8. annoy   8. ounce

1. a void   6. moun tain
2. oys ter   7. our selves
3. roy al   8. al low
4. em ploy   9. some how
5. an noy   10. a mount

Page 55
These words should be circled.
1. spoil   6. amount
2. royal   7. somehow
3. avoid   8. ourselves
4. oyster   9. annoy
5. ounce   10. boundary

These words should be circled
and written correctly.
1. enploy   howse
   employ   house
2. choyse   mountin
   choice   mountain
3. moysture   grownd
   moisture   ground
4. Sumhow   ownce   umount
   Somehow   ounce   amount

Page 57
1. a. one whole word
   b. words separated with a
      hyphen
   c. two separate words
2. goalkeeper bodyguard himself
   everybody   everyone   themselves
3. first aid
4. birthday
5. everybody   everyone
6. good-bye   outside
   something   (or anything)
   everybody   (or everyone)
Sentences will vary.

Page 58
outside
birthday
high school
good-bye
himself
something
all right
airmail

1. first aid   a
2. flashlight   i
3. one-way   a
4. everyone   e
5. maybe   a   e
6. anything   e
7. baby-sit   a   e

Page 59
These words should be circled.
1. baby-sit   6. one-way
2. first aid   7. birthday
3. flashlight   8. good-bye
4. all right   9. anything
5. airmail   10. high school

These words should be circled
and written correctly.
1. first-ade   goal keeper
   first aid   goalkeeper
2. allright   birth day   air-mail
   all right   birthday   airmail
3. bodygard   flashlite
   bodyguard   flashlight
4. Evrybody   out side
   Everybody   outside

Page 61
1. daughter   awkward (or awful)
2. author   drawn
3. lawyer   already   office
4. always   brought
5. called   because

Sentences will vary.

Page 62
1. stalk   9. office
2. off   10. although
3. because   11. awkward
4. brought   12. already
5. called   13. daughter
6. drawn   14. lawyer
7. haul   15. author
8. belong

1. awful   5. always
2. awkward   6. belong
3. fault   7. haul
4. author   8. off

1. awkward, awful
2. author, always
3. haul, off

Page 63
These words should be circled
and written correctly.
lawyre/lawyer   ask/asked
becawse/because   dotter/daughter
ofice/office   brote/brought
awkword/awkward   awfull/awful
draun/drawn   fawlt/fault
all ways/always

Page 65
1. surrounded   carried
   studied   worried
   bragged   worried
   finished   laughed

2. skiing   swimming

3. a. finished   e. quickest
   b. traveling   f. laughed
   c. weaker   g. bragged
   d. worried   h. tinisest

Sentences will vary

Page 66
1. laughing -   no change
2. loving -   drop e
3. beginning -   double final
                 consonant
4. skiing -   no change
5. swimming -   double final
                 consonant

1. surrounded - no change
2. studied -   change y to i
3. traded -   drop e
4. carried -   change y to i
5. excited -   drop e

1. quickest   3. weaker
2. lonelier   4. tiniest

Page 67
These words should be
circled and written correctly.
braged   bragged
sking   skiing
laffed   laughed
begining   beginning
exsiting   exciting
worred   worried
travling   traveling
qwickest   quickest
finish   finished

Page 69
across   down
  4. women   1. countries
  5. leaves   2. calves
  6. addresses   3. guesses
  8. people   5. lessons
12. skis   7. fences
14. cherries   9. friends
15. flies   10. families
16. businesses   11. lives
                     13. roofs

Page 70
1. skis - add s
2. countries - change y to i
   and add es
3. fences - add s
4. leaves - change f to v and
   add es
5. roofs - add s
6. flies - change y to i and
   add es
7. lives - change f to v and
   add es
8. families - change y to i and
   add es
9. guesses - add es
10. pictures - add s
11. calves - change f to v and
    add es
12. lessons - add s

1. women   5. oxen
2. cacti   6. moose
3. mice   7. deer
4. octopuses   8. feet
   or octopi

Page 71
These words should be circled.
addresses
lessons
friends
leaves
fences
families
businesses

These words should be circled
and written correctly.
1. womun   lessuns   peopel
   women   lessons   people
2. adresses   frends   countrys
   addresses   friends   countries
3. busnesses   pitchers   familees
   businesses pictures   families
4. calfs   cherrys
   calves   cherries

Page 73
across   down
  3. certain   1. camera
  6. remember   2. purpose
11. cold   4. earth
12. doctor   5. smuggler
14. surprise   7. mayor
15. Thursday   8. color
                 9. wonder
                10. thirsty
                11. collar
                12. dollar
                13. person

Page 74

urgent Thursday smuggler
thirsty earth surprise
collar certain person
camera color dollar
wonder purpose early
doctor mayor

/ər/ spelled 6 ways

1. ur	y	1. urgent
2. thirst	gler	2. thirsty
3. won	gent	3. wonder
4. smug	ly	4. smuggler
5. pur	tain	5. purpose
6. col	der	6. collar
7. cer	pose	7. certain
8. may	prise	8. mayor
9. ear	lar	9. early
10. sur	or	10. surprise

Page 75

1. urgent   6. mayor
2. camera   7. person
3. earth   8. doctor
4. dollar   9. early
5. wonder   10. color

These words should be circled
and written correctly.
1. mayir   erly   Thursday
   mayor   early   Thursday
2. irgent   thirstee
   urgent   thirsty
3. cirtain   docter
   certain   doctor
4. persun   remembre perpose
   person   remember purpose
5. smugglar kamera   doller
   smuggler camera   dollar

Page 77
1. dictionary
2. dairy
3. a. orchestra
   b. partner
4. a. beware d. guarding
   b. daring e. force
   c. argument
5. a. large   b. before c. ordinary
6. a. square d. large
   b. daring e. force
   c. beware f. before

Sentences will vary.

Page 78

/a/ in fair	/ar/ in car	/or/ in store
square	argument	orchestra
dairy	large	important
stare	partner	force
ordinary	guarding	before
area	article	ordinary
January		
dictionary		
daring		
beware		

1. argument   6. dictionary
2. beware   7. article
3. partner   8. before
4. orchestra   9. ordinary
5. important 10. daring

Page 79
These words should be circled.
stare   area
partner   daring
article   argument
orchestra

These words should be circled
and written correctly.
1. fource   garding   orkestra
   force   guarding orchestra
2. inportant artikle   january
   important article   January
3. Bewair   argumints lawrge
   Beware   arguments large
4. areeu   sqware
   area   square

Page 81
1. equator   different
2. hospital   animal
3. algebra
4. happen   again
5. puncture
6. region   quiet
7. lecture   quarter

Sentences will vary.

Page 82

algebrǝ   happěn   hospitǝl
brother   animǝl   secǝnd
weapǝn   along   regiǝn
thousǎnd   agǎin

Page 83 (continued)
1. a bout   10. punc ture
2. oth er   11. thou sand
3. weap on   12. qui et
4. hap pen   13. al ge bra
5. a long   14. dif fer ent
6. re gion   15. e qua tor
7. quar ter   16. hos pi tal
8. sec ond   17. a gain
9. lec ture   18. an i mal

Page 83
These words should be circled
and written correctly.
kwiet   quiet
animle   animal
rejun   region
lechure   lecture
ubout   about
equater   equator
puntured   punctured
weppon   weapon
hapen   happen
allong   along
hospitel   hospital
secunds   seconds
agin   again

Page 85
1. a. athletes c. children
   b. watches d. chocolates
2. a. purchases
   b. watches
   c. exchange
3. rhythm
4. thought   athletes   truthful
   though   rhythm   together
   arithmetic months   length
5. a. awhile   d. though
   b. where   e. exchange
   c. thought   f. white

Page 86
1. awhile   10. purchases
2. thought   11. though
3. exchange   12. friendship
4. rhythm   13. length
5. chocolates   14. white
6. watches   15. children
7. where   16. arithmetic
8. athletes   17. months
9. truthful   18. together

1. months   4. chocolates
2. athletes   5. watches
3. children   6. purchases

These words should be circled.
women   children

Page 87
These words should be circled.
athletes
together
awhile
length
though
exchange

These words should be circled
and written correctly.
1. atheletes   munths
   athletes   months
2. childrn   arithmutic
   children   arithmetic
3. perchases   choclates
   purchases   chocolates
4. frendship   thought
   friendship   though
5. exchanj   waches   wite
   exchange   watches   white

Page 89
across   down
  3. decided   1. signals
  4. circle   2. peaceful
  6. bridge   3. dangerous
  7. figure   5. energy
  9. generous   8. genius
  12. since   10. electric
  13. segment   11. concert
  14. regular
  15. nice
  16. country

Page 90
1. g   1. k
2. j   2. s
3. j   3. s
4. g   4. k
5. j   5. s
6. g   6. s

1. coun try   8. danc ing
2. sig nal   9. gen ius
3. peace ful   10. dan ger ous
4. seg ment   11. gen er ous
5. fig ure   12. e lec tric
6. cir cle   13. reg u lar
7. con cert   14. de cid ed

Page 91
These words should be circled.
dancing   country   signal
energy   segment   figure
regular   electric

These words should be circled
and written correctly.
1. cuntry   pieceful
   country   peaceful
2. dangirous   brige
   dangerous   bridge
3. genrous   sinse
   generous   since
4. dansing   cirkle   concirt
   dancing   circle   concert

Page 93
1. terrible   eagle
   (or frequent)
2. instrument
3. several   celebrate
   (or special)
4. Address   label
5. special   telescope
   (or instrument)
6. whole   little
7. example

Sentences will vary.

Page 94
1. eagle   6. whole
2. towel   7. several
3. special   8. label
4. example   9. little
5. legal   10. terrible

1. spe   quent   1. special
2. ques   dress   2. question
3. fre   clare   3. frequent
4. in   tion   4. instead
5. de   cial   5. declare
6. ad   stead   6. address

1. ex   ri   ble   1. example
2. sev   e   al   2. several
3. ter   e   ple   3. terrible
4. cel   am   brate   4. celebrate
5. tel   stru scope   5. telescope
6. in   er   ment   6. instrume

Page 95
These words should be circled.
special   celebrate
question   telescope
address

These words should be circled
and written correctly.
1. Sevral   terible
   Several   terrible
2. eegle   teleskope
   eagle   telescope
3. towle   speshul
   towel   special
4. qwestion   insterment
   question   instrument
5. uddress   lable
   address   label

Page 97
1. a. tried   c. tired
   b. hurried   d. planned
2. their-Sentences will vary.
3. a. weigh b. their c. piece
4. a. not either
   b. surrounding a place for
      the purpose of capturing i
   c. measure how heavy
      something is
   d. a piece of land used
      for crops or pasture
   e. intense; savage
   f. one part of a whole thing
   g. feels concern

Page 98
long a   long e   long
weigh   piece   tried
              receive   tryin
              field   writir
              neither   tired
              siege

1. receiving - drop e; add ing
2. write - drop e; add ing
3. planning - double final consonant
4. worry - no change

1. received - drop e; add ed
2. worried - change y to i; add ed
3. planned - double final consonant
4. tried - change y to i; add ed

Page 99
These words should be circled and written correctly.

tryin	trying
feerce	fierce
seige	siege
feilds	fields
neithur	neither
piese	piece
They're	Their
havving	having
worrys	worries
tarred	tired
writting	writing

Page 101
1. a. teacher
   b. actor
   c. liar
   d. biologist
   e. assistant
2. honestly   exactly
   speedily   happily
3. c
   d
   a
   e
   b

Sentences will vary.

Page 102
1. darkness   3. weakness
2. loneliness 4. happiness

1. honestly   3. friendly
2. angrily   4. speedily

1. sad ness   5. exact ly
2. teach er   6. lie ar
3. happy ly   7. lonely ness
4. kind ness 8. act or

Page 103
These words should be circled.

biologist	sadness
honestly	happiness
speedily	exactly
kindness	darkness
teacher	

These words should be circled and written correctly.
1. lyer honistly
   liar honestly
2. teecher frindly
   teacher friendly
3. biologest's assistent speedyly
   biologist's assistant speedily
4. acter exacly darknes
   actor exactly darkness

Page 105

across	down
1. byte	2. through
4. principal	3. clothes
10. reign	5. chute
11. heir	6. principle
12. sub	7. hour
14. scene	8. cruise
16. aloud	9. write
17. they're	13. bell
18. isle	15. crews

Words not on list-sub, bell

Page 106
1. scene   9. aloud
2. reign   10. hour
3. through   11. two
4. they're   12. byte
5. cruise   13. isle
6. principal   14. clothes
7. write   15. knew
8. heir   16. chute

long e	long a	long i
scene	they're	byte
seen	reign	isle
		write

long o	ow	oo
clothes	aloud	through
close	hour	cruise
		knew

Page 107
These words should be circled and written correctly.

seen	scene
princepal	principal
close	clothes
threw	through
our	hour
too	two
cruise	crews
principel	principle
Their	They're
crews	cruise

Page 109
1. b   6. f   11. k
2. d   7. h   12. l
3. e   8. g   13. m
4. a   9. j   14. n
5. c   10. i

Sentences will vary.

Page 110
1. careless   4. useless
2. excitement 5. government
3. thoughtful 6. plentiful

1. care less   5. a muse ment
2. waste ful   6. won der ful
3. thought less 7. ex cite ment
4. plen ti ful 8. suc cess ful

Page 111
These words should be circled.

careless	worthless
thoughtless	useful
reckless	excitement
arrangement	

These words should be circled and written correctly.
1. usless   carless
   useless   careless
2. arranjment   amusment
   arrangement   amusement
3. wreckless   punichment
   reckless   punishment
4. goverment   sucessful   peeceful
   government   successful   peaceful

Page 113

across	down
1. caution	2. no
4. official	3. fiction
6. conclusion	5. constitution
8. sugar	7. musician
12. constellation	9. physician
13. addition	10. patience
14. can	11. tension
15. shoes	15. sure
16. glacier	

Words not on list-no, can

Page 114

1. shoes	5. official
2. glacier	6. addition
3. caution	7. sugar
4. sure	8. position

/sh/ spelled 4 different ways

1. fic	ar	1. fiction
2. sug	sion	2. sugar
3. pa	tion	3. patience
4. mis	cier	4. mission
5. gla	tience	5. glacier

1. phy	clu	cial	1. physician
2. con	fi	tion	2. conclusion
3. of	di	sion	3. official
4. ad	si	cian	4. addition

Page 115

These words should be circled.

shoes	musician
caution	official
glacier	tension

These words should be circled and written correctly.

1. shure	shoos
sure	shoes
2. missun	glasher
mission	glacier
3. pacience	musition
patience	musician
4. fysician	tenshun
physician	tension
5. conclushun	ficshun
conclusion	fiction
6. oficial	possition
official	position

Page 117

1. a. wrong	c. often
b. answer	d. listen
2. a. knapsack	b. tonight
3. a. wrong	c. often
b. answer	d. listen
4. unknown	
5. a. dough	c. half
b. island	d. whistle

Sentences will vary.

Page 118

1. wrestle	7. half
2. answer	8. whistle
3. often	9. tonight
4. climb	10. island
5. talking	11. design
6. knot	12. scratch

1. wrong	5. knapsack
2. unknown	6. write
3. listen	7. bomb
4. limb	8. calf

1. wrestle -	short vowel
2. often -	schwa
3. climb -	long vowel
4. listen -	schwa
5. half -	short vowel
6. answer -	short vowel
7. dough -	long vowel
8. knapsack -	short vowel
9. island -	schwa

Page 119

These words should be circled and written correctly.

islend	island
napsack	knapsack
talkin	talking
tonite	tonight
anser	answer
climmed	climbed
limm	limb
not	knot
doe	dough
scrach	scratch
desine	design
wrawng	wrong
restled	wrestled

Page 121

1. a. illegible	
b. misspell	
c. disappoint	
d. rebuild	
e. misfortune	
f. misuse	
2. a. do again	
b. not	
c. bad	
d. not	

Sentences will vary.

Page 122

1. disappoint	4. illegal
2. misbehave	5. misunderstand
3. rebuild	6. disappear

1. dishonest	4. disapprove
2. disagree	5. illegible
3. illegal	6. disconnect

Page 123

These words should be circled.

recover	disappoint
illegal	illegible
dishonest	recall

These words should be circled and written correctly.

1. rebiuld	misfortunate
rebuild	misfortune
2. rekall	disconect
recall	disconnect
3. desapprove	missbehave
disapprove	misbehave
4. mispell	ilegible	reright
misspell	illegible	rewrite

Page 125

across	down
2. paragraph	1. nephew
5. telephone	3. physical
8. few	4. festival
10. pharmacy	6. enough
11. cough	7. trophy
12. triumph	8. fragile
13. briefly	9. fourth

Page 126

1. paragraph
2. few
3. trophy
4. telephone
5. enough
6. nephew
7. briefly
8. roughest
9. pharmacy
10. festival
11. cough
12. stuffed
13. fluid
14. physical
15. fragile
16. triumph

1. trophy
2. enough
3. pharmacy
4. fluid

5. fragile
6. few
7. triumph
8. briefly

1. trophy   triumph
2. fragile   pharmacy
3. briefly   enough

Page 127
These words should be circled and written correctly.

trophee   trophy
triumf   triumph
friday   Friday
neffew   nephew
Festtival   Festival
phisical   physical
frajle   fragile
Breefly   Briefly
ruffest   roughest
enuf   enough
forth   fourth

Page 129
1. imperfect
2. impolite
3. inactive
4. impatient/unable
5. unaware
   impolite/inconsiderate/
   improper
   uncomfortable
6. preview/prehistoric
7. incorrect/prefix
8. prevent/prejudice
Sentences will vary.

Page 130
1. imperfect
2. prejudice
3. incorrect
4. uncertain
5. preview

6. prevent
7. inconvenient
8. prefix
9. unaware
10. impolite

1. imperfect
2. impolite
3. unaware
4. inactive
5. ungrateful
6. impatient

7. inconsiderate
8. prehistoric
9. uncomfortable
10. inconvenient
11. unable
12. improper

Page 131
These words should be circled.

prevent   imperfect
unaware   inconsiderate
prehistoric   prejudice
uncertain   prefix
inconvenient

These words should be circled and written correctly.
1. impolight   inkonsiderate
   impolite   inconsiderate
2. prevue   perhistoric
   preview   prehistoric
3. uncomterble   unsertain
   uncomfortable uncertain
4. unawear   perfix
   unaware   prefix

Page 133
across
1. geologist
4. bicycle
6. cyclone
9. autobiography
12. automobile
13. telegraph
14. enact

down
2. geography
3. transport
5. encyclopedia
7. portable
8. action
10. photograph
11. import

Page 134
1. geo+ology=geology
2. auto+bio+graph=
   autobiography
3. trans+port=transport
4. photo+graph=photograph
5. act+tion=action

Page 135
These words should be circled and written correctly.

automatick   automatic
encylopydia   encyclopedia
geogruphy   geography
automobeles   automobiles
geomtrie   geometry
geollogy   geology
autobiografy   autobiography
portabel   portable
emport   import
transprot   transport

Page 137
1. decorate
   decoration
2. punctuate
   punctuation
3. destruct
   destruction
4. administer
   administration

5. populate
   population
6. infect
   infection
7. attend
   attention

Page 138
1. destruction
2. infection
3. attention
4. description
5. decoration

6. administration
7. population
8. division
9. punctuation

1. de struct
2. di vide
3. des crip tion
4. dec o rate
5. in fec tion
6. pop u late

7. punc tu ate
8. at ten tion
9. ad min is ter
10. dec o ra tion
11. punc tu a tion

Page 139
These words should be circled.
description   describe
decorate   population
attention   punctuate
infection   destruct
administration

These words should be circled
and written correctly.
1. discribe   decorashun
   describe   decoration
2. devide   admenestration
   divide   administration
3. atention   puntuation
   attention   punctuation
4. populacian   infectted
   population   infected

Page 141
1. vertical   7. currency
2. amphibian   8. atmosphere
3. intersection   9. civilization
4. agriculture   10. substitute
5. frequency   11. equation
6. semicircle   12. temperature

Sentences will vary.

1. multiply   10. semicircle
2. vertical   11. technology
3. equation   12. temperature
4. currency   13. amphibian
5. frequency   14. intersection
6. atmosphere   15. environment
7. substitute   16. agriculture
8. characteristic 17. civilization
9. representative 18. manufacture

3 syllables
vertical   substitute
equation   currency
multiply   frequency
atmosphere

4 syllables
temperature   agriculture
amphibian   manufacture
intersection   semicircle
environment   technology

5 syllables
civilization   representative
characteristic

Page 143
These words should be circled
and written correctly.
1. amfibian   envirunment   temperachur
   amphibian   environment   temperature
2. equasion   mulltiply
   equation   multiply
3. civilisation   agrikulture
   civilization   agriculture
4. atmusphere   characturistic
   atmosphere   characteristic
5. representuteves semycircle
   representatives semicircle
6. substutute   kurrency
   substitute   currency
7. manufacter   intersecton
   manufacture   intersection